DON'T LEAVE

8 Years of Working with Teddy Riley, Blackstreet

& Future Recording Studio

By

Anthony Rolando Brown

Foreword

You got your problems baby I've got mine...before we get into any of the problems let me take your mind back waaaay back, the year was 1991 and I was two years out of the army, just graduated from the Department of Defense Police Academy been convicted of a federal crime and was living in a halfway house. Yeah I know that's s lot to take in but it set the stage for what would become nearly 7 of the most influential years of my life. Years of working for one of the top music producers of the time. A producer who was sought out by artists from every genre of music...greats such as Patti LaBelle and Michael Jackson to up and coming artists who never got a chance to make their mark in the industry everlasting. In 1991, I began an internship with producer Teddy Riley who was just starting his own record label Future Records.

That internship would eventually lead to a full time job and promotion to the title of General Manager and eventually me leaving. One of the most fascinating phenomena I observed while working in this wonderfully weird world of music was the assumption by those holding power that everything is replaceable and people are interchangeable.

Fuck the soul and passion that a person has about their art or job, if it fits the program but the person doesn't guess what...your outta here buddy. Being in charge of personnel, part of my responsibility was hiring and firing employees and trust me we went through a few but on the artists side it was Teddy who would cut the cords. If a person no longer fit into Teddy's dream that person was more than likely about to have a rude awakening, which was the case with a few of the member of the group BLACKSTREET and part of my motivation for writing this book. The other part is to leave a memoir of my life as part of my legacy to my family especially my children Anthony Jr, Chiara, Danielle and Cameron.

CHAPTER 1

The Foundation

I was born to a single mother named Alma Brown on December 22, 1964 in a city called Portsmouth Virginia. My father, whose name was Abram Martin, was a police officer in Newark New Jersey. Like so many other fathers in the 60s, he was non supportive and wasn't around as I grew up. It was just me, my mom and my younger sister Annette. My Grandmother Gertrude "Sister" Brown helped my mother raise me and Annette and as we got older my aunt Vivian would watch us. We moved around a lot when I was young between Ida Barbour where we lived, Prentis Park where my Grandma lived and Jeffrey Wilson where my aunt lived, I basically grew up in every project in the city. I never met my father Abram until later in life. When I was 45 years old he sent me a Facebook friend request. My first thoughts were "damn I hope he doesn't need a kidney", nonetheless I got a chance to meet him eventually. I had a number of great male role models growing up. I learned early life lessons from my great uncles who were my grandmother's brothers, like James Abbott Watson (the War hero), James Herbert "Poo Cat" Watson (the Pimp), Nathaniel "Baby Ray" Watson (the ex con brawler) and my mother's brother Robert Brown who is my favorite uncle taught me everything mechanical while my uncle Emmanuel Brown and cousin Mike Watson taught me style and gave me a love for music. I had a number of great men who would often impart their advice and wisdom upon me. Portsmouth, was home to a lot of talented people such as Jazz Legend Ruth Brown, fashion designer Perry Ellis, comedian Wanda Sykes and more recently music stars such as Missy Elliot, Chad Hugo and Shay Haley but I'll touch more on those last three later. As a kid I always had a glimmer of glitz in my eye. My cousin Michael was a doo wop type singer who went to I.C Norcom High School and was in the school's marching band. My entire family attended Norcom which was the city's black high school.

By the time I attended high school in 1979, I went

to an interracial school called Manor High School where I participated in sports such as Football, Track, Wrestling, Tennis, Soccer and eventually was selected to be the captain of every team I played on. I had a natural leadership nature in me that others noticed too. In addition to sports I joined the school band and played in orchestra, marching band and several neighborhood bands. I loved music from as early as I could remember and had a knack for rhythm. I started out in band playing a flute that my cousin Michael had given me but after a few jokes on how "sissy" the flute was I switched to the trumpet. Playing brass instruments and boxing wasn't a perfect combination and a busted lip caused me to switch to the drums and percussion. I was a good drummer and played the timbale in the marching band. The timbale gave the drum section that funky melody. I would march at halftimes of football games in my football uniform which pissed off everybody. The band kids were like "he gets to march in his dirty uniform and we have to be clean and crisp" while the football players were like "why does he get to skip the halftime ass chewing we get from the coach?" My high school football coach Tony Morrison understood band was a grade for me and would let me participate. Hip Hop was just taking full form in the 80's. My best friend in high school was named Vincent "Dinky' Pugh. Dinky's brother Michael was a senior my freshman year and also a hot DJ. I joined up with him and a group of popular band members from Manor High School, Ronald "Dr. Feelgood" Woods and Michael "Master Blaster" Pugh who had formed a DJ group which was called "THE PORTSMOUTH ALLSTARS". Back then we would have community DJ battles against DJs from other neighboring cities. In Chesapeake we had "Big Bad Bass" "Bobby Roscoe" and in Norfolk we had "The Controller". The point of the battle was to drown out the other DJs sound, pull the crowd over to your set and wow all the honeys. My job back then didn't wow too many honeys as all I was doing was carrying plastic milk crates full of records from the van to the inside of the venue. But I was hanging with all of these cool older cats getting schooled on basic hood entertainment 101. My fascination with and love for music kept me locked in.

I was always the type of kid who would read every word of an album cover, all of the credits. I wanted to know who recorded what, where...who the session musicians were, who the writers were, what equipment they used and everything, so to me carrying crates of records was like an advanced indoctrination program. I was also the youngest of the bunch at 14 hanging around adults gave me a lot of exposure into their world especially the night-life..our parties would always be packed. By the time senior year rolled around I was the father of a 2 year old son and trusted enough to DJ a party BUT, only during the slow song sets. You see, Feelgood and Blaster would like to go grab a girl and slow dance for like 4 songs but I would cut the songs short, play a fast song and turn on all the lights.

It was embarrassing to some guys because they would pull away from the girl and they would be on the hard with penis prints poking through the baggie slacks…Blaster would HATE that. "Damn Tony play all 4 of the songs man." He would fuss at me but they never tried to fight me …I was told

I was crazy. One particular time we were DJ'ing a party at the Cavalier Manor Gym, earlier that summer I had visited NYC and seen a DJ scratch for the 1st time... as usual I was playing the slow song set standing in the DJ booth watching all the cool guys slow grind on girls and decided to end the slow song set by scratching in the song "Planet Rock" "Doon doon doon doon doon ziggy ziggy zigga" This time both Blaster and Feelgood ran over to the set "What the fuck are you doing trying to ruin my needles?" Feelgood yelled at me and examined his turntable, everyone else thought I was playing bad vinyl. Those were my early musical foundations. From there it only grew and my experiences would be amazing and priceless. Never in a lifetime would I have thought I would meet over half of the artists whose records were in those crates and befriend a lot of them.

Portsmouth Allstars at The Cavalier Manor Gym 1982

CHAPTER 2

The Horizon

My next summer would be spent in Basic Training for the United States Army at Ft McClellan Alabama. Initially I hated the Army during that basic training phrase but after I started to learn the actual skills associated with my occupation I began to love it. I qualified expert with all assigned weapons and went through additional training related to anti-terrorism and hostage negotiation after-which I was assigned to a Military Police Special Forces Unit in Vicenza

Italy working with the 1/75th Ranger Battalion. I fell in love with Italy and it was mutual.

I stayed in Europe until 1989 and I must say my time in Italy was absolutely amazing. Aside from the initial culture shock I experienced arriving during the Carnival period, (seeing a man dressed as a nun wearing fishnet stockings and shade glasses riding a Vespa had me fucked up for a minute), I settled in pretty well overseas. I made a lot of friends in the Italian community which I never expected.

I lived off base and my Italian neighbors loved me. They would invite me to dinner almost daily and teach me how to cook their food, speak their language and assimilate to their culture. I excelled at my military duties and received promotions quickly.

I was one of the youngest Non Commissioned Officers on post and quickly became a squad leader. Most of the other squad leaders were already in their 30s and I was barely 21 years old. The post where I was stationed had a tackle football team. I wanted to play college football immediately after high school but like I said, I had a kid whom I loved and I chose to be a responsible father and be able to provide for my kid and at that time the military was the best choice. My first Sergeant gave me permission to try out for the team. If I made the team, I would have some exemptions from my regular duties. So, I joined the base's football team and played wide receiver.

We played against other branches of the Military and other bases in the region and soon had Pro Scouts from the IFL (Italian Football League) selected me to play Professional Football for a team in Northern Italy called the Warriors.

Our base commander thought this was a great community relations tactic so he allowed some of the soldiers to participate in the IFL.

To me it was great because I was getting paid more money from one week of playing football than one month of being in the Military.

After winning the Championship, the Italian equivalent to the Superbowl our team went out to this nightclub called the "Hippodrome". The place was jammed packed with sexy ass Italian chicks and the music was a mix of loud techno beats and what sounded like some form of European House music. I was in full celebratory mode standing on chairs spilling champagne on women when the DJ fucked up and played "Rapper's Delight" by the Sugar Hill Gang. At this point I was totally feeling myself and I grabbed the microphone from the DJ booth and rapped the WHOLE song American Style!

People went wild and within minutes I was approached by an Italian Music Producer named Massimo..."Hey Man That was fucking cool man" Massimo exclaimed in the best english he could muster. "Hey Man you wanna make a record man?" he asked as he pulled out his business card. "Hell yeah I wanna make a record!" I said, placing his card in my pocket. The following Monday, I went to meet Massimo who pitched me a great and fantastic opportunity. An opportunity that I had never asked for nor had even imagined...Massimo gave me a recording contract.

The entire contract was written in Italian and about 15 pages thick. I knew how to speak some words in Italian but I did not know how to read it... but the numbers on the advance check were in dollars and I understood that very well. Massimo told me to "take the contract to you base and show you master, we can't do business with American Soldier unless your master says so. " MASTER?!? I aint got no damn master what the fuck you talking about?" I responded standoffishly but we worked things out. Because of the communication gap, Massimo didn't know the correct word was "Supervisor" but, he did not have any ill intent using the wrong word. Nonetheless, I took the paperwork to several people on base to review, my 1st Sergeant, my Company Commander and even the Base Interpreter Gianni, but each of them was more impressed by the check for $25,000 which was stapled to the last page of the contract. I signed the contract and returned it to Massimo about 4 days later at which time he gave me another check for $25,000...I hadn't even cashed the first check yet.

I was thrusted into the studio that same weekend and wrote and recorded 10 songs in 2 days after which Massimo gave me another check, but this one was for $50,000. Now I had more money than I had ever seen at one time in my life. Up until then, the most money I had ever seen at one time was $800 and I had to pull one full month of military duty to get that. I went into the studio and wrote songs to a bunch of "Euro" beats Massimo had selected but I wasn't feeling them and wanted to add more American Hip Hop feel into the music. I eventually ended up recording a solo project as "Tony B and The Electric Warriors"

A year later I recorded a duet with another

Photo of Tony B and The Electric Warriors

American named G.Q. Jay an Italian guy named Enrico Santacaterina, and a German guy named Christian Hornbostel to form the group VENICE and a top 10 single with the song titled "Hello DJ"

We were an Italian an American and a German in our 20s with great hair and a hot song ripping up the Italian Rivera. Sex on the beach takes on a whole different meaning when two Italian super models are involved. Ah life was good.

I would pay other off duty soldiers who just wanted to hang out in the barracks $100 to pull my military duty while I went off doing music shit. I would make good money doing shows at clubs and opening up for major artists at concerts and festivals and soon brought a brand new

Japanese sports car, which was rare because, Italy did not import cars from Japan at the time. So I would trade my Nissan for Massimo's Ferrari from time to time because he wanted to show off in a ...well a foreign car.

One day, I was pulling up to the studio and I noticed the cars in the parking lot. I noticed my keyboard player had a Porsche, Pipi my guitarist had a Maserati and there was Massimo's Ferrari and here I was in a Nissan... I asked the keyboardist Christa, how did you afford your car? She mentioned a magic word one that I had never heard before, but a word that bothered Massimo so much that his ass levitated across the room to interrupt the conversation. That word was "ROYALTIES".

My music was making noise overseas and aside from the $150,000 I received as an advance ($100,000 in 3 payment instalments and $50,000 in studio, video and production cost) I hadn't received any money from the sales and radio play of my music. I had been performing almost nightly at clubs in Europe, been on Italian and German National TV shows and had songs certified gold, but was not entitled to receive royalties..."It was all in the contract" Massimo tried to explain to me but his explanation wasn't good enough so I sought out a better response and wanted to learn everything there was to know about the proper ways to get paid in the music business. I was done with recording and being pimped.

I went from being an artists to being an employee at the same label I was signed to and learned the behind the scenes workings of the music industry. Since the label I was on was a CBS affiliate we had offices on the lower floors of their building in Milan. I was in Milano working part-time in the promotion department of CBS Europe so I got a lot of perks like VIP tickets to see all the CBS acts when they came to Italy. Working there gave me the chance to have an after concert dinner with singer Al Jarreu in a small Italian restaurant where he started scat singing and beating on the table, attracting a small crowd. I also had the opportunity to meet Michael Jackson for the first time and to see him perform at every venue in Italy.

When I first met Michael Jackson it was 1988 at a CBS Records meet and greet, where we all stood in a line as he passed by and shook all of the employees in my department hands. I was the only black guy there so of course he noticed me. "Are You an Italian" he asked as he passed me. "No, I'm from Virginia," I replied as I shook his hand. "Virginia..Cool" he replied as he continued down the line. Those were 5 of the most memorable seconds ever. After being rushed out of the door we all went back to work prepping for his Bad Tour debut in Rome.

Michael Jackson's concert that night was spectacular. I had never seen anything like it in my life. The stadium was jammed packed and people were actually hanging from the street lights and rafters. I spent 7 days from May 22 til May 29 of 1988 rolling through Italy in support of the tour.

I wish I could say I was chilling with Michael but after that meet and greet the only other time I ever saw him was on stage. I would get to the tour city the day before and set up promotional items at radio stations and at the venue then hang around until the concert.

Attending concerts in a VIP capacity was one of the best perks about working at the label but soon the Italian CBS offices were closed down. The company was bought out by Sony and jobs were being replaced. I returned to the United States reluctantly and somewhat against my will, because I loved Italy. I had a dope ass condo in Milan an apartment near Venice and a lot of beautiful women, 2 Christinas, Antonella, 2 Daniellas, Nicoletta and Francesca, plus I was well connected in that country with everyone from political figures, and military personnel to fashion designers and corporation owners... even mob bosses, like my girlfriend Francesca's father Don Rovaldi.

Seniore Rovaldi was an older Italian man with fingers as thick as sausages and a big meaty Italian nose. He made it very clear to me the first time Francesca had taken me into their home that he was skeptical about his daughter dating an American especially a Black American and tried to do some type of tough guy scare routine on me, but I was from Jeffrey Wilson housing projects in

Portsmouth Virginia , my uncles were Poo Cat and Baby Ray, I wasn't scared of this guy he wasn't the muscle...his sons on the other hand were trouble. We worked well together though and manage to make a lot of extra money on the side by smuggling diamonds from Africa to New York... but that's a story for another book. Bottom line is Italy embraced me and I embraced Italy, but it was time to go.

Chapter 3

Back to The U. S of A

When I came back to the United States I had a wealth of knowledge and understanding about the internal workings of the business and while attending the Department of Defense police Academy, I started my own production company on the side from the dining room of a small apartment I had on a back street in Portsmouth Virginia. My job in the Military had been that of a

Military Police Officer and Special Reaction Team Anti/Counter Terrorist Team Leader, so my natural inclination was to seek the same type of work or something similar after I got out of the military and until I could rejuvenate my musical interests. You gotta work a real job while your dreams are manifesting and I did. I worked my ass off but nothing could fill that void from the money and admiration I had in Europe.

Fame is a hell of a drug ...even a little taste of it distorts your reality. In Europe I was a football star and music celebrity earning money running errands for the Italian mob and getting a government check from the Army. I missed all of that...especially the money.

The work I did in the military was very different from the bullshit that the civilian police did and I was not happy with that type of job. Even after being an honor graduate from the police academy, I wasn't feeling that type of work in the civilian world, so I quit and did the next best thing to making money. I started taking money...I couldn't run diamonds for the Italians anymore so, one of my Jewish buddies from the diamond runs showed me a new hustle where we would take credit cards from rich kids through the mail and intercept the PIN numbers.

Once we had the PIN numbers we would then withdraw cash from the accounts. We went through hundreds of cards, before I got caught with one. I got stupid and sloppy and went into a department store to buy a suit for my Grandmother's funeral and the clerk noticed the name on the card ...Kaydo Matsumodo ..."Funny, You don't look Japaneses" she said while silently alerting the police. We were getting so much money off those cards and it was so easy to do. This was in an era before cameras were everywhere and even the cameras they had and were using were pieces of shit.

I was eventually charged with a Felony in Federal Court, sentenced to 4 years. There were a few other things that occurred during this period that do not have a statute of limitation, therefore I wont get into detail, but your boy was grinding and what I was arrested for was the least of my crimes at that time, so I'm grateful to have escaped the worst of it.

Towards the end of my sentence, I went to live in a half-way house on 20th Street in Norfolk called RSI which stood for "Rehabilitative Services Incorporated". My hope and ambition was overwhelming and I was not trying to stay in that halfway house at all. Loopholes: the feds would allow me to leave the halfway house if I was enrolled in a training program or going to work…so I did both. I got my man Blake, a Jamaican from England who was living in Virginia to give me a job on paper as a concert promoter with his company "Infinity Promotions" and I enrolled FULL TIME in college at Norfolk State University, then I got a night job editing TV commercials and tweaking satellites receivers for a cable company in Chesapeake Virginia called Tidewater Cable Interconnect.

This schedule pretty much kept me out of the halfway house and busy. Working with Blake was cool. He was a very private person, a lot of people thought he was into drugs, but I think he just came from money and found a fun way to flip it by promoting concerts. Working at Infinity allowed me to leave the halfway-house daily and go to a nice lil high rise office suite in Virginia Beach where I would make calls to this guy in New York named Erskine Issac to book artists to come perform in Virginia. I learned a lot about negotiation from working around Blake and Erskine...."If your first offer doesn't insult the person it wasn't a good offer" Blake would always say...so I would call up Erskine and ask to book an artists like Shabba Ranks for $5000.00 it never worked but it got the ice broken.

Blake and I promoted a lot of concerts in and around Hampton Roads Virginia in every sized venue from skating rinks to stadiums. We would do a lot of ground level promotions leaving tickets on consignment in clothing stores and record stores around Hampton Roads Virginia. While working at Infinity I had enrolled in college and was going to school full time at Norfolk State

University where I was studying Pre-Law and Mass Communications.

College was a great place to be a concert promoter, I had tickets to all the hot events and would often have access to the artists once we booked them and brought them into town. I would often drive them to the radio station to do on air interviews leading up to the event. Around this same time I was still recording my own music project with friends I had before leaving for the Army. Troy Mitchell, John Mitchell, Gerald Austin Barry McNeal and Henry Wynn were members of 2 of the hottest rap groups in the area Prophets of Rage and Black Culture. After some time and a few sessions at MitKar recording studio in Norfolk a decision was made to create the music group 3 Feet which consisted of brothers Troy and John Mitchell, Gerald Austin as emcees and Henry Wynn as the DJ Plus One. 3 Feet eventually earned the attention of Salt-N-Pepe founder Hurby "Love Bug" Azor. Azor secured a deal for the group on London Polygram Records.

The first rap group from Virginia to get a major label record deal. Once Hurby and his crew (DJ Wiz of Kid and Play and another producer named Dre) secured 3 Feet's deal we were invited to come live in Queens NY and begin production of the album. I tried to share a lot of insight to the business based on what I learned in Europe with the whole royalty debacle and for a while the group looked as if they would be on point.

We spent a lot of time in the studio working on Salt -N- Pepa songs like "Shoop" and "What A Man" in fact it's the voices of 3 Feet's that give the song its iconic intro "yeaeeee ohh yeahh yeaaaaaa". From there we went on to do major television shows like David Letterman, Saturday Night Live and the ESPY Awards but only in support of Salt-N-Pepa's new album which bothered Troy. "I'm not Salt-N-Pepa's background singer" he would exclaim "I'm ready for our shit to come out". Troy's aggression frightened niggas and label CEO Peter Koepke eventually dropped the group from London Polygram.

Chapter 4

Headed To The Future

Meanwhile and simultaneously I was finding more and more creative ways to escape the halfway house. Work and school took up the majority of my day and I was barely spending any time at RSI but by my senior year at NSU I was a father of 3 and needed to get money. Thanks to great people such as the president of NSU Dr. Harrison Wilson giving me recommendations I had been released early and had more freedom to move about.

I wanted to pledge Omega but they had been kicked off campus and Dr. Wilson pulled me to the side and said "You don't need to be in a frat, I read your file, you were an elite soldier, and an ex cop before you went to jail all these young knuckleheads are they're going to do is piss you off trying to tell you what to do, and you'll find yourself in trouble again." I listened to the wisdom he dropped on me and forgot about fraternity life and dove into the books.

The 1st semester of my senior year I had a great professor, Dr, Wanda Brockington hook me up with 2 amazing internships. I did a summer long internship at Spike Lee's 40 Acres and A Mule, where he was nearing the completion of the Malcom X movie. I helped out in the wardrobe department, but my curiosity caused me to snoop around and visually learn as sets were being made, cameras were being loaded, scripts were being edited on the fly and adsorbed it all. My second internship was with Teddy Riley at Future Recording Studios in Virginia Beach VA. This would be the internship that would change my life. Someone once said "There's no better education than to learn from the Masters" and I had two of the biggest teaching me. Teddy was just setting up shop in Virginia and had been here for less than a full year when I started my internship.

I was more excited about the internship at 40 acres, because I wanted to work in film since I had already worked around major record labels, but the proximity of Future was the main attraction... My family is all here in Virginia. I remember having to walk from Norfolk State University which was in Norfolk Virginia all the way to

Virginia Beach to meet Teddy at Future Recording Studio. I had a car, but since I was in the halfway house I was restricted from driving.

I was in good shape so it wasn't as bad as it would be if I had to do that today. I met with Teddy in private for about an hour and we talked about music and studio stuff. He was very friendly and child-like...meaning he had a level of excitement that was like a kid with a new toy or something. He smiled the whole time and seemed surprised at how much I knew about working in recording studios and like he was impressed with my knowledge of music technology.

I had worked with sequencing and sampling which were new techniques used in production at the time, I knew how to load a 2 inch recorder and splice tape. Plus I knew how to work computers and digital editing software. Teddy was sold .

You'd never guess it but "yep yep" Teddy has a computer nerd buried inside of him. After our talk he introduced me to Donna Moore who was his manager at the time. Donna then introduced me to Nicole Rembert, a very attractive and down to earth young lady who at the time was the girlfriend of his brother Markell Riley. Teddy's operation was divided between two locations back then. He had the "Office" which was located on South Plaza Trail and the "Studio" which was located off of Virginia Beach Blvd.

Virginia Beach Blvd is a major road in the city but the studio was barely visible from where it sat, off the road behind a Vet clinic. South Plaza Trail is nestled off of Independence Boulevard near Mount Trashmore. Teddy's live-in girlfriend and mother of his daughters was Donna Roberts who sometimes worked in the office too, but Nicole

Rembert ran the office and was responsible for paperwork and answering calls, communicating with the label and accountants and such PLUS she made the meanest sandwiches ever. "What did Teddy say he was going to have you do?" Nicole asked me...."He said he wanted me to organize the gear in the back room and do some A&R work" I replied... "I told him about the work I did overseas and here with Infinity and he wanted me to do some A&R stuff for him" I explained to Nicole, she led me to the back room of the office which was being used as a huge storage space, and turned on the lights.

I immediately noticed all of the boxes strewn about...it was boxes and boxes of all kinds of shit. Costumes and clothes from GUY's last tour, cables, wires, gadgets all sort of stuff. Near the door on the right side of the wall, was a huge box that once held a floor model television set now jammed full of cassette tapes of people who had sent demos into Teddy for consideration. "Those are some of the demo tapes people have been sending in " Nicole explained "Have Fun".

I stepped back and looked around and thought to myself "they're just trying to get me to clean up this room...", It was bewildering. So I began the task of screening demo tapes from thousands of submissions. I found demo tapes that had been dropped off from Richmond R&B singer DeAngelo, I found demo tapes from Missy Elliot's first group "Sista" I found demo tapes from Timbaland and Pharrell when they were in a group called "Surrounded By Idiots" and so many more that hadn't even been considered but just tossed in a box.

I actually found a demo tape from "3 Feet" that I

had dropped off a year earlier to Teddy's then brother in law Omar Chandler (RIP). Finding that tape jolted me a little. I went to Teddy at the studio and had a talk with him..."Hey Teddy man I dropped this tape off last year did anyone even go through these tapes?" Teddy was surprised that nothing had been getting done and turned the A&R demo department over to me.

I took it so serious. I actually listened to each and every tape in that box in order to be fair and objective. I wanted to impress him with the selections I was choosing for him to review. Once I got a good selection, I took them over to the studio for him to review.

Teddy was in fact so impressed, that he asked me to set up a showcase and invite the artists I selected. I began the task of typing rejection letters and sending people their tapes back and preparing letters of interest inviting artists who had good music on their tapes to come perform for Teddy at Future. Then I would call all of his label executive friends and invited them down to Virginia to review the showcase. THE TEDDY RILEY NIGHT OF MAGIC SHOWCASES

The first year we did the showcase it was small and only a handful of artists performed. We held the showcase which was more of a live listening session in the studio but it was not long before the idea grew. I suggested that we turn that listening session into a talent showcase. Teddy knew I was good at event planning through the work I did with Infinity so he gave me the green light to start promoting "THE TEDDY RILEY NIGHT OF MAGIC TALENT SHOW".

Teddy's cousin Lucy Washington helped me with the logistics. Lucy was a great people person and a woman of God, she was the perfect counterbalance to my hot-headed demeanor. She was cool and tolerant. I contacted the local radio stations to get the ball rolling. I had a lot of connections at the local stations because NSU had a radio program and a lot of people who came through the Mass Communication program worked in radio and I brought a hell of a lot of radio advertisements as a concert promoter.

So when I went to them with anything Teddy Riley related they were all ears. Lloyd Vaughn Jr. was the sales rep I dealt with to put out the call for artists to audition for the main showcase, but soon the station's promotion manager got involved and the event became huge. The response was incredible. We had thousands of singers, rappers and musicians audition to be in this showcase but we only had slots for a few acts.

So Lucy, Nicole, myself and Lucy's brother Christo began pre-screening performers for the showcase. The first event was held in the auditorium at Princess Anne High School, which was a local high school in Virginia Beach about 3 blocks away from the recording studio but by the following year the popularity of the event had grown so large that the whole city of Virginia Beach became involved. Mayor Myrea Obendroff (RIP) came on board to make it a City wide spectacle.

I negotiated the rental of the Virginia Beach Pavilion and set up a bunch of activities between the staff at the studio, radio station and city to make the event huge and successful. We had celebrity basketball games, softball games and bowling matches, concerts, talent shows and artists showcases where recording industry professionals came in to scout talent from

Virginia. I wanted to do an event like Jack The Rapper or Peter Thomas' and "How Can I Be Down" I had already promoted successful events at Freaknik and around Hampton Roads so this should be simple.

These "Teddy Riley Talent Showcases" that I put

Photo from 1st Teddy Riley Talent Showcase

together were definitely the predecessor to Pharrell's "Something In The Water Festival" which took place in 2019.

It felt good to live long enough to see certain things come full circle. Pharrell went from sitting on the floor in Teddy's studio watching an event taking place to hosting and organizing his own years later.

Once I had all of the locations in place, I invited vendors and every label executive in my rolodex to attend and using Teddy's name was the main draw. Blake and Infinity came in and booked all of the side events and after parties.

Chapter 5

Surrounded By Talent 1991

I met Pharrell, Mike Etheridge, Chad Hugo and Shay Haley at the front door of Future Recording Studio around 2:30 in the afternoon one day. I wasn't even working at the studio yet, but I was over there handling some business when the doorbell rang. I opened the door to a group of young dudes who wanted to meet Teddy but the one who stood out was wearing a metallic silver bubble goose coat and ski goggles. "Hello is Mr Riley Available" …."Teddy there some kids out here wanna talk to you" I relayed their message but Teddy wasn't interested at the time. "I'm sorry Teddy is busy at the moment" I'd returned with the news. This happened a few times until they finally made their way in…enter the Neptunes. Nobody else will tell you this but Teddy did not like the overall dynamics of the Neptunes as a group act. He took more to Mike Etheridge who was the R&B singer of the group and he used Chad Hugo to play sax over a few tracks, but a lot of times he would tell us not to even open the door for Pharrell.

From one perspective this could be seen as fucked up, but to his defense in most cases when Pharrell popped up Teddy was busy working other times he just didn't want to be bothered. I think

Pharrell's persistence annoyed Teddy a little but definitely paid off for him. Pharrell, Shay, Chad and Mike were all cool lil dudes to me. They were like the Virginia Beach offshoot of the native tongues.

At the time, Teddy had Tony "Sifu" Watts working

Big Bub, Heavy D, Sifu Watts, Teddy Riley and Guest in the A Room

as his personal security and bodyguard.

Sifu is a martial arts master and Wing Chun Instructor, we took an immediate liking to each other because of our similar military background and training in martial arts. Sifu used to hold

Wing Chun classes at his home in Virginia Beach and Chad and Pharrell were among the students training there.

I was a certified practitioner and would assist Sifu and his brother Ty from time to time with his classes helping to train his new students and becoming his Martial Arts Disciple. I've seen him dismantle multiple attackers in real life street and bar fights and throw a guy through a nightclub window, then jump through the glass and continue to whip his ass.

To this day, Sifu is still what you call a baaaaad man. His kids Tony David Marcus and even his daughter Crystal were all nice with it too. I would jokingly tell Chad Hugo ."Chad you already got a physiological advantage looking like Bruce Lee". Sifu which is actually a Chinese word for "teacher" became a big brother to me. In time, Mike E left the Neptunes for a solo career and got signed to Capital where he released a solo album.

Meanwhile, the remaining members of the Neptunes were still hobnobbing and rubbing shoulders looking for their break.

I spent a lot of hours in the office developing general procedures, filing documents, clearing samples, and communicating with the parent labels like MCA and later Interscope. I applied what I learned working overseas and absorbed even more from the employees on the other end of the phone who worked for the parent labels. Nicole and I set up the Wreckx-N-Effect fan club which was about the most bullshit thing I was part of while working there. It was fun to read the fan mail, but I spent hours signing autographs for Markell, Teddy and Aqil onto W-N-E publicity photos and mailing them out to fans, "Nicole what the hell are these guys doing that they can't come and sign a few of these their self?" I asked she responded "probably over at the studio shooting dice or playing video games." But that was a celebrity privilege and part of why I was even there so I didn't complain.

I just figured out creative ways to make my Teddy Riley autograph look different from the Markell Riley autograph which had to look different from the Aqil Davidson autograph.

After a while Teddy brought in fashion designer and his own personal stylist Kareen Linton. Kareen was a beautiful brown-skinned sister from Barbados via New York with a knockout figure and sexy island accent. She was also a beast when it came to fashion design and clothing manufacturing. She had gained some mass notoriety designing clothes for celebrities Martin

Lawrence, LL Cool J and Positive K. By the time Kareen came to the office I had the back room pretty cleared out and we converted it into her design space where she would make custom pieces for the groups. It was fun painting the "T.R. Face" logo on the back wall.

My fondest memory with her was taking her and her daughter Christmas tree shopping and just hanging out together in a strictly platonic relationship we bonded and became very cool.

A lot of celebrities were endorsing or starting their own clothing line during this era and Teddy and Kareen started L.O.R. Wear. A clothing line inspired by Teddy but designed by Kareen. She could have been on a major level like Fubu's creator, but something fell through and that's her story to tell. So here I was sitting in an office full of beautiful women, but not one time did the thought of flirting with them cross my mind.

I respected Riley's girlfriend's Nicole and Donna Roberts, because they were more like wives than girlfriends to them and I came to think of them both as sisters.

I respected Donna Moore as a mentor. She confided in me a lot more than I was ready to receive, but her information and the talks we had were priceless. Donna Moore gave me a foothold there. One day Teddy's brother Markell walks in as we were all having lunch.

Markell sees me in the office surrounded by women and less than an hour after his visit I got a phone call from Teddy…"Tony I want to move you over here with me"… So I packed up my lil desk putting everything into my leather briefcase and file cabinet, left the office on Southport Plaza and moved over to the Studio on Virginia Beach Blvd.

Chapter 6

Tony Brown from the Office

As soon as I arrived at the studio I was greeted with a loud yet cheerful southern voice yelling out "TONY BROWN FROM THE OFFICE" exclaimed Tim Smith. I walked into the front door of Future to see Tim standing there with a few guys I had never seen but then there was Bobby Brown who was in town for some reason.

I was surprised at how cool Bobby was. He was married to Whitney Houston (RIP) at the time and when she walked out into the hallway I low key lost it inside. I was a big Whitney Houston fan, but I tried to always stay cool and not freak out around these celebrities despite their musical accomplishments. Bobby and Whitney were so also very approachable despite their enormous celebrity status. Maybe because the studio was such a restricted environment. Whitney was a doll and my "You married the wrong Brown joke" made both of them smile.

What surprised me is when I found out she smoked. I was standing outside smoking a Newport when she walked up behind and asked for one. "Sure" I said offering her a smoke and lighting it for her. From time to time she would step outside to smoke a cigarette, I would join her and just chat "I wish I had a joint" she whispered to me I laughed and by the next cigarette break shared a joint on the side of the building with her...I ended every conversation with her by saying my silly joke "you know you married the wrong Brown don't you"

Now once I got to the studio, Tim and I quickly bonded like brothers. He was a slim brown skinned well groomed guy from Columbus Georgia and cool as a fan in January. "Come on let me show you around this joint" Tim gave me the "working man's" tour of the studio showing me all of the equipment closets and storage spots.

Studio Manager Tony Brown in the A-Room of Future Recording Studio

The place was a mess for real and while I initially thought Markell and Teddy wanted to get me away from their women, I understood what my purpose there was to be. "Tone you've been doing a good job at the office. I want to make you the studio manager." Teddy told me…"These guys around here seem to respect you and you are great at organization. Do whatever you need to make my studio work." GREEN LIGHT!

First thing I needed to do was bring some order to the place. The inmates were running the joint. Up until that day I had only popped in and out of the studio to have Teddy sign something or brief him on something. The dynamics of the building were very different from the office. At the office we did business, it was relatively quiet and I was home by 6pm. The studio was an eclectic mix of everybody and their momma. Dancers, singers, rappers, musicians, producers, runners, engineers, writers and wanna-bes …everybody was at the studio and the schedule was 24/7.

Lucy had been working at the studio doing light tasks so again I looked to her for help. I needed to know everything about the place in order to manage it properly so we started with inventory. I created a computer database which tracked each piece of equipment and developed a bar scan code system to check equipment in and out of the studio.

We put barcodes on all of the keyboards, microphones, anything that wasn't nailed down was documented and tagged. It was a pretty sophisticated system for the time and it allowed me to know where every piece of equipment was. Which was handy whenever Teddy went on a rampage and wanted all of his equipment back.

We would often let artists sign out keyboards, drum machines and equipment to work on their own at home. One particular time Teddy wanted all of his gear back in the studio because he was looking for a particular piece and couldn't find it.

Whenever it was time to go repo equipment Teddy sent me to do the job. I was like a damn henchman going around to people's houses and studios repossessing audio gear. Once I showed up at Pharrell William's house to pick up some gear Teddy had let him borrow but suddenly wanted it back.

Pharrell was so distraught that he started crying at the front door.

He was passionate about his craft and I guess he really needed that keyboard or was upset that Ted was taking it back. "Man look as soon as Teddy leaves town come sign this shit out again man…he just wanna inventory his shit you know how he is" I tried to offer him some comfort because it was fucked up to have someone give you something then ask for it back.

I made sure Pharrell got the keyboard back after

Teddy laid his eyes on it.

The repo shit had gotten so bad that it would stress relationships with people I liked and had no problem with, like when I tried to pick up some equipment from Leon Sylvers, he challenged me to a fight.

Leon was my man and I looked up to him as a mentor of sorts. We were both martial artists and he was a bassist and would show me licks from time to time. I felt bad about going to get the gear but Leon was pissed…"I ain't giving Teddy back shit ..lets fight for it" Leon proposed that we fight and If he won he could keep the equipment …he ended up giving me the equipment. And no, we didn't fight, we had mutual respect for one another and were able to talk about a solution. He knew I was just doing my job.

There were a number of people who I had to go

repo keyboards drum machines and equipment from like Tony and Jody, but unlike Leon Sylvers I didn't have the same level of respect for them and was going to fuck them up in their own studio but I had learned earlier from a conversation with Teddy's former manager Gene Griffin ..."ALL THAT SHIT IS INSURED if you lose it or break it, so what? Order a new one". So I would sometimes "loose" gear after it came back off tour, especially if it was band equipment, because in most cases it would be all beat up and shit. So I would sell it off as used, file a claim for missing equipment and order brand new equipment in time for the next tour.

The guys at the local music store AL&M loved to see me coming in the door. They knew I was going to drop a few thousand dollars of record company money on new keyboards or MPCs. Aside from organizing the studio I had to deal with the personalities of the individual working there. On one side you had the Georgia Boys: Sprague Williams, the equipment tech turned producer. Tim Smith, the manager, Walter "Mucho" Scott, Daryl 'Dezo" Adams (RIP), Lil Chris Smith, a dope upcoming producer and Marcus "Slim" Vance. Dezo, Mucho and Slim were all members of the group Basic Black. Basic Black was another New Jack Swing group established by Gene Griffin after the group GUY broke up. Sprague was a producer and Tim was their manager.

On the other side we had the New York Boys which included: a whole lot of dudes from a crew called "Posse Deep" and the Davidsons, Big Al Davidson (RIP), Idris Davidson, Aqil Davidson of Wreck -N- Effect, Tone Capone, Chris "Christo" Washington and Lee "Big Bub" Drakeford of the group "Today". Tension would build up between these two groups and from time to time escalate into minor fights.

Everybody rocked with their crew and when something jumped off internally you rode with your crew…there was the epic battle between Walter "Mucho" Scott, a cock diesel Georgia boy and R&B singer with Basic Black vs ex-NYPD officer and Teddy's big cousin Christopher "Christo" Washington. Christo was a huge proponent the martial arts and held a Black Belt in Harlem Go-Ju Karate. Like myself and Tony "Sifu" Watts we all loved martial arts. It was one of those testosterone filled days and Christo and Mucho's shit talking began to get to each of them. From my perspective, Christo was the agitator in this instance and Mucho had been repeating the phrase all black people say when they are trying to avoid trouble…"go head man… go head man". Christo's Karate didn't work much against Mucho's muscle and the scenario ended with me pleading with Christo to "give me the gun" after Mucho scooped him up slammed him down then gave him those hands, Christo fought his way up and went to retrieve a sawed off 12 gauge shotgun which eventually became mine. "Bro c'mon give me that" Christo gave me the gun and Mucho left. Another internally violent situation pitted a few Posse Deep members from Harlem against Lil Chris Smith, a producer from Columbus Georgia that left Lil Chris hospitalized with head trauma.

This was a bad situation because even though he wasn't from Virginia, Lil Chris had gained a lot of friends while he was living in Virginia and knew a lot of cats in the hood. He had love in the hood especially with my boys from P-Town. So after the hood got word that some guys from New York attacked Lil Chris a plan was made by people who rocked with him to get revenge and take out Aqil Davidson from Wreckx-N-Effect. Aqil was the "high profile guy" from NY the main reason any of them Posse Deep dudes were even in VA but Aqil was my friend too. It was crazy because a group of guys from Virginia were ready to ride against a group of guys from NY for something that happened to a Georgia dude while his homeboys from Georgia stayed in the cut and didnt do anything.

When I got wind that they wanted Aqil I immediately put the brakes on that plan. "Man yall stupid? You can't do anything to that dude without serious repercussions. Lil Chris got people from Georgia they gotta handle that for him". Lil Chris got out of the hospital eventually and went back to Georgia. The guys who put him in the hospital had already returned to NY. I don't know if the guys from up North thought the guys from down South were slow, but I often found myself refereeing between the two groups. Wreckx-N-Effect "Rump Shaker" which was released in 1992 was one of the hottest songs of the summer and Teddy had been doing a lot of dates with Aqil and his brother Markell but a lot of R&B cats were always around, writing and recording demos. The studio was an eclectic environment and everyone initially seemed like they were up to something sneaky.

The only people I trusted at first were Nicole Rembert and Donna Moore; they were straight shooters. Nicole only had Markell's best interest at mind even if it meant going against Teddy. That the real definition of ride or die. Donna wanted to do good business but felt like she was being played.

Chapter 7

My first job after college (1993)

By May of 1993 I had graduated from Norfolk State University with a Bachelor of Science degree in Mass Communication Television & Film Production and was ready to enter the working world.

1993 Norfolk State Graduation Photo

While my marriage to my wife Zina had all but fallen apart amidst accusations of me sleeping with groupies, to actual acts of infidelity. We separated and eventually divorced but, I had 3 kids at the time all by her that I was financially, emotionally and morally responsible for so I had to get to work. I had a pending job offer on the table from every place where I had completed an internship while in college.

I had job offers from 40 Acres and Mule and WTKR, a local television station. Both businesses made substantial offers but Teddy stepped to me and simply said "I'll pay you more than they are offering to stay here at Future" and like that my decision was made. My first job following college was as the A&R Director for Future Records. Nicole had ordered me some fancy silver metallic business cards and I gave them away like they were burning my pockets.

During this time Teddy's personal project was a new group he was putting together post GUY called BLACKSTREET. The group consisted of Joe Stonestreet, Chauncey Black, Teddy Riley and Levi Little and the song they were pushing at the time was for the soundtrack of Chris Rock's movie CB-4 and entitled "Baby Be Mine". Teddy had also just finished the Wreckx-N-Effect album and people often questioned if he was a member of the group or not after the success of "Rump Shaker". For the "Baby Be Mine" video, Teddy gave me a shot to do a lot on this project, thanks to Donna Moore. I researched a bunch of directors who had videos playing on BET or MTV to select the production company and choose a director for the video.

We built a set in an alley in Downtown Norfolk that I had used as a backdrop for a few rap videos

I shot for local artists and before long production was under -way. I thought the video was good but they did a second version in LA.

Chapter 8

Where Do Joe Go

Joe was the First To Go. Joe Stonestreet was a phenomenal vocalist, his tone and clarity were impeccable but his private life was not as bright. Joe was a wild boy when Teddy wasn't around but as with most people he was a little more reserved in TR's presence.

I always wondered about that...why were people afraid to be themselves when Teddy came around? I remember once at Teddy's birthday party in Miami we were on the yacht smoking weed and every time Teddy came topside Aaron Hall from Teddy's old group GUY would toss the joint overboard….Nigga you wasting good weed! Nonetheless, people tend to "act" some type of way in Teddy presence.

Joe was boisterous and I could tell right off the bat that he had a problem with substance abuse. If you've ever lived in the hood you know how certain people act and to me Joe acted like a cool ass feign. I used to see Joe around before I knew he was in the group.

The group name "Blackstreet" was initially a combination of the last names of Chauncey Black + Joe Stonestreet = BlackStreet. Just think, using that naming logic we could have had a group called "Blackstone" or StoneBlack but Blackstreet seems to work fine. After Joe left, Teddy came up with a new explanation for the group's name. He would explain to people that He (Teddy) is from the streets of Harlem and Chauncey was... well just black. That became the post Joe Stonestreet explanation in interviews whenever asked about how the name came about.

Joe tore up the vocals on the single "Baby Be Mine" which is the only song on the debut album which featured his voice on the leads. Making the video was an all day event and I was running around until the very last minute making props like the "Blackstreet" street sign at the 24 hours Kinkos, filling up water trucks for rain effects and fetching flashlight batteries, but it was so exhilarating...not quite as exhilarating as the first video I experienced working at Future Records, which was the video for Wreckx-N-Effects' hit

"Rump Shaker" I was still working at the business office location when that video was shot.

The rump shaker video auditions had bikini clad women lined up for about 4 blocks trying to get a spot in the video. I think the video we did in Norfolk for Baby Be Mine was too gritty for Hollywood because they soon flew the group to Cali to re-do the video with nearly the same treatment we had for the initial video except the stook a few clips from the movie CB-4 into this version. By the time either of the videos for "Baby be Mine" were released, so was Joe.

No one had to tell me anything I knew drugs were part of the reason Joe was asked to leave the group. Teddy had a strict policy about drugs, even weed. I had a homie who used to sell to Joe and I had seen him and interacted with him before I even knew who he really was. When Joe started to see me around the studio and office he would give me a silent vibe of (Don't tell this nigga Teddy my business) and I never did. I knew what Joe was into but it wasn't my business, I was new to this circle, as far as I knew they all might be doing coke. I still feel like some sort of an intervention would have been warranted instead of just kicking him out. You know, do something to help that man get his life back on track, but it never happened.

What followed next for Joe was a series of bitter interviews and lacklustre performances in front of small lounge sized crowds where he'd sing Blackstreet songs like "No Diggity" which he didn't even record on or have anything to do with. Shit was sad.

So, I walk in the studio one day ready to get my work day started and there is this dude sitting in the lobby who introduces himself to me as Dave Hollister and says he's waiting for Teddy. I went into the A-room which was the main recording studio room at Future , Teddy was on the phone giving me the hold up finger and when he finally hung up he excitedly asked "did you meet Dave he's the new guy"..."New guy in what?" I asked "Blackstreet" Teddy said, smiling as he walked out to get Dave and bring him back into the A-Room.

Teddy gave the order "Go get the reel for Baby Be Mine, we're putting Dave's voice over Joe's". "Psst...Yo Teddy kicked Joe out of the group..Joe kept fucking with that stuff...No no Joe left because he wanted more money" the whispers around the studio began but regardless of the reason, Joe Stonestreet was out and being replaced by Dave Hollister.

I reached out to Joe about a week later just to fish for his side of the story but all I got was a "Fuck that nigga Teddy."

On Monday June 25, 2018 Joseph Ephraim Stonestreet passed away at the age of 56 in his hometown of Cincinnati Ohio.

My first impression of Dave was a good one he exuded confidence and swagger and when I heard him sing I knew where those characteristics came from. God had blessed this dude.

Chapter 9

1993 Blackstreet Album One

By late 1993, with Dave in place, recording on the album began. This was an energetic atmosphere with writers, producers and performers all submitting ideas and music for the first Backstreet project. Even I had a few song ideas floating around my head, but I wanted to stay focused on managing the studio. As studio manager part of my responsibility was scheduling sessions to make sure everyone could get the studio time they needed and I was also responsible for maintaining equipment and inventory, making employee schedules and hiring and firing people. Tim Smith became my assistant manager, he had a lot of sense and some experience managing Basic Black. Tim became my right hand and was instrumental in helping the place run. Teddy placed the care of the studio in my hands and was able to focus on his creativity. From time to time he would have me terminate a few people for one reason or another. It could be something simple like firing a housekeep because he didn't like the way she vacuumed the floor or he would ask me to fire a person if he suspected them of doing something. Like the time Teddy lost his gun and thought my assistant Keivan stole it. I always felt bad when I had to tell someone that they were fired but, I would always try to make sure they got a more than fair severance pay. I fired one guy so much we gave him the nickname "Higher Fire". That guy was Teddy's personal assistant and cook, Earl Thomas. WHA GON ON STAR? That was Earl's standard greeting to almost everyone he met. Earl was probably the oldest guy on staff, he was a studio runner who always stayed up under Teddy. He was a whimsical guy from Trinidad who spoke with a melodic accent and could cook his ass off. Earl also dabbled in beat making and production and would often be in the B-Room tinkering around on the equipment. People would walk and be like "What the hell is Earl in there doing" but, magic struck and Earl landed a song on the soundtrack of the movie "Blankman". As we began the pre-production phase writers such as Tammy Lucas and Leon Sylvers began to frequent the studio more. Tammy Lucas was one of Teddy's female protegees. She was a lovely lady with an absolutely amazing voice and her 1992 song "Is It Good To You" from the Juice soundtrack was a standout. I always thought that Teddy would release her as a solo artist after the success of that song but it never happened...I mean we went through the motions and I still can't think of a reason why she wasn't released aside from some folks who did not know how to market her image at the time. Leon Sylvers was from the legendary group The Sylvers, who had a series of hits in the 70s and 80s like "Boogie Fever" and "Hot Line" and my favorite "Misdemeanor". I had known about them from back when I was a kid. Leon was a cool and very approachable. Leon loved to play basketball. This dude had a mean jump shot and overall game and he was a martial artist, but his real passion was for music and I notice unlike a lot of the other producers Leon did a lot of work from his home studio, which was smart considering the hourly rate we were charging at the time. Eric Sermon from EPMD came in to work on the song "Booti Call" and then the remixes started pouring in.

Tammy Lucas, Pharrell and Chad came in with a banger that became one of my favorite songs on that album "Tonight's The Night" and Tammy Lucas sang her ass off on this beautiful duet but by the time the video came out she had been replaced by Coko from SWV and Craig Mack had been added.

People such as Lil Chris Smith, Ty Fife, DJ Wynn Big Bub, Tom Taliaferro all contributed their time and talent to the creation of this classic. But the engineers...the engineers are the ones who polished everything up. When I first started working for Teddy at his business office, his studio was being ran by Keston Wright who was the lead engineer, Jean Marie Horvat was another engineer who was around the studio in the early days, but for whatever the reason the time came to replace them.

I sat in interviews with Teddy and the new engineers coming in Serban Ghena, John Haynes and George "Junior" Mayers. When I met Junior he walked into the A- Room to meet with me and pulled out a 9mm handgun and placed it on the console. "I carry my gun with me…is that going to be a problem?" Junior said. I responded by pulling out my .45 and a small 380 pistol and placed them on the console and saying "I don't see why as long as you don't have a problem with it". We both laughed our asses off and became instant buddies. To this day Junior and I still hang out and have become brothers.

John Hanes was a red headed white guy with glasses. He was the quiet wholesome type but John liked guns too. In fact everybody in the studio was strapped. I even had a bullpup shotgun mounted on a swivel under my desk. You know just in case.

And then there was Serban who was a tall dark, handsome foreign looking guy, with a jet black mullet, he looked like he was from one of those Eastern European countries. Serb was brilliant, I was impressed by an invention he showed me of a bass guitar with retractable frets ...pretty cool. Serb also had a hunger to learn every engineering technique and how to operate the mixing console that he would sometimes sleep in the studio UNDER THE CONSOLE like he was on the bottom bunk and he would carry the operators manual to the new SSL mixing console home to study it.

I knew all about consoles, computers, drum machines, sequencers, samplers, how to mic instruments, how to slice and edit 2 inch audio tape every piece of equipment in Future Recording Studio. I had hands-on experience working in major recording studios in Europe back when I was an artist. I would sit at the console with Serban and go over things with him. Fast forward years later to present day, it absolutely blows my mind that Serban would go on to win more than 10 Grammys for engineering and has mixed and engineered over 100 number one singles.

That's a hell of an accomplishment after leaving the Future, but Serban left Future Recording

Studios with a chip on his shoulder ...so did John... so did Junior...eventually they would all leave but I'm still in 1994 so let's get back on track.

Serban would catch a lot of flack for fucking with

Tim Smith, Tony Brown, George Junior Mayers

settings that Teddy left a certain way whether he did it or not he got blamed. I would try to save all of the mixer and sound settings whenever Teddy left or went to sleep, so that whatever he did last would be recalled automatically. I was deep into computers and showing other studio employees how to do certain tasks on the computer.

One of those people was Teddy's cousin Lucy Washington. Lucy caught on fast and had a knack for paying attention to detail that some would call being nosey. So some of the guys would avoid Lucy because they thought she was reporting back to Teddy. For example they would be a group of guys gambling shooting dice in the pool room but if Lucy came in they would stop. Stuff like that. Her and her brother Christo were cool to me and they too soon became like family. Even though they were Teddy's blood relatives he would often put me in the uncomfortable position of firing them or rather breaking the bad news to them that they were being fired.

There were a lot of Teddy's friends from New York and Family members who he gave odd jobs to around the studio. It was his way of looking out for them, but making them earn it at the same time. One such guy was Allan Davidson lovingly known as "Big Al". Big Al was actually a cousin to Aqil and Idris Davidson and had grown up with Teddy in St. Nick projects up in Harlem, New York. Big Al was my man 100 grand, he was a 6 foot 5 teddy bear who rolled with W-N-E everywhere they went. Big Al was like a moderator. He would always step in whenever Aqil and Teddy would have an issue and try to negotiate a resolution but no mistaking it he would ride or die for Aqil. Big Al had a lot of respect for how I took care of the studio and would always tell me with his heavy New York accent "Tone you doing your thing son".

Al was somewhat devastated by how Wreckx-N-Effects would eventually be dismantled at the hands of Teddy and he and I had a number of lengthy conversations about how he could keep Wreckx-N-Effect going. That brother loved what he did for them; he loved the group and the members of the group and relished in their success. Moreso Big Al loved Teddy Riley despite his disdain at Teddy's choices and actions. Sadly, Al took his love for WNE, Teddy Riley and New Jack Swing to the grave. I was surprised that neither Teddy nor Markell attended Al's funeral but I drove from Virginia to New York to attend Big Al's funeral in 2017 and pay my respect to my homie.

At the funeral I caught up with a few of my New York guys from the studio, Aqil, Idris, Mutay, Earl Thomas, Tone Capone. Tone Capone was another of the guys from New York who rolled with Wreckx-N-Effect. Anthony Pollard, more known as Tone Capone was Markell's right hand man, floating around Virginia Beach in a purple mini van. The infamous purple Mazda MPV.

Everyone in the Hampton Roads area knew that vehicle was associated with Teddy Riley Wreckx-N-Effect and Future Recording Studios. Tone Capone was a very handsome dark skinned brother about 6'3" with a smile that literally lit up a room. Tone was a flashy NY guy always well dressed with a mean sneaker game.

Tone was on payroll but I had no clear definition of his position...he was Markell's man. Around the studio and would later just be chilling with Jigga whenever I saw him. Whenever Teddy took Tone Capone off payroll Markell looked out for him. Tone loved basketball and if he wasn't out in front of the studio shooting hoops he would either be chilling playing a video game or gambling or bringing girls through...Black, black dudes love redbones. Tone Capone had all the pretty light skinned girls up in the Mazda. It used to be funny to hear him and Chauncey joke about who was the darkest. DeAuthur Dixon was a friend of mine from Portsmouth who managed to marry into Teddy's family by wedding his sister Niecy. Naturally Teddy gave his brother in law a job. DeAuthur had a job as a runner at the studio and part of a runners responsibility was cleaning bathrooms, taking out trash and running errands. DeAuthur got mixed up in the shenanigans of all the women coming in and out of Future and caught a wandering eye.

Niecey was not having that neither was Teddy so DeAuther Dixon was one of the people I broke the news to..."Teddy is not going to need your services after Friday bro". Thing is, DeAuthur had no intention of working anyway. He was still going to be good because Teddy wasn't going to let his sister suffer financially so as long as she was good DeAuthur was good. He definitely had a moochers mentality.

Omar Chandler was another one of Teddy's brother in laws who was most noted for his powerhouse vocals on Rob Base hit "Joy & Pain" Omar was a celebrity who was employed by another celebrity and I think his focus was more on developing and growing his career rather than digging through boxes of demo tapes. Omar was actually the first person I met from Future. One night my boy Troy Mitchell and I had driven up to Teddy's new studio to hand him a demo tape and Omar was in the parking lot smoking a cigarette. I recognized him from the video "Oh shit Omar Chandler" I said while dapping him up. "I wanna drop off this demo of my man Jason Alias" I told him handing him a cassette tape. "Jason Alias huh it better be some fire" Omar replied.

The demo tape WAS fire but Teddy never got a chance to hear it. Troy had gotten a deal with another label and when I first started working at Future in the office on Southport I found that same cassette in a box of demos. Omar was a good writer himself and was working on his project at the time I first arrived so I'm thankful he didn't have time to go through that box of demos. That actually gave me a lot to do.

In 1991 Omar released his self titled album Omar Chandler on MCA records. In 2013 I received the news that Omar was murdered in his studio by a group of artists whose career he was trying to help advance. "Joy & Pain, is like sunshine and rain." There were a lot of faces around, everyone was either being creative or wanting to contribute to the creative process. By 1994, when it was all said and done, the first Blackstreet album was complete.

The group had already undergone a personnel transition and the eyes of the R&B world was upon Teddy Riley's new post GUY group.

The first album contain the following songs: "Baby Be Mine" which was an uptempo dance tune where Joe Stonestreet initially sang leads but was replaced by Dave Holister. Lil Chris Smith, a producer from Columbus Georgia, provided the main groove for this song. Lil Chris practically lived in the studio inside of the B Room. He was ambitious, he wanted to be on every song and remix every thing and I always had to stay on his ass about keeping the spot tidy and picking up after himself.

Back then producers kept their sounds on 3.5 inch floppy disks and would carry a case full of disks with different drum sounds and stuff. Chris would leave shit all over the place and take sounds from Teddy's disks. I had to start locking up Teddy's sounds in a file drawer until he needed them.

The track "U Blow My Mind" was a good mid tempo song where Teddy starts on leads in almost a Stevie Arrington tone (Stevie was the lead singer from the group Slave) but eventually all of the members would chip in.vocally with Levi growling ad libs and Chauncey wailing along while Dave sings a run of riffs. Levi was and still is one of the coolest cats I know. I have a lot of respect for him as a man and artist.

On the song "I like The Way You Work" Chauncey Black leads vocals and the song was one of my favorites. It's one of the ones that I witnessed grow from the concept to the completion. It was magic that started with one person just nodding his head to a beat that only he could hear in his mind and became a hit.

On the song "Good Life" Teddy sang leads in a monotone style but the group held the song together for what would be a decent album cut. "Good Life" was produced by DJ Wynn and Teddy the song borrows from the familiar melodies of T.S. Monk's hit song "Bon Vie"

Another banger was the song "Physical Thing". On this song Chauncey Black pours it out as he sings the lead on this song. The song itself had a catchy sample from Gangster's "92 Interlude" which in itself was based on the song "Young Gifted and Black" by Aretha Franklin. It was an educational experience clearing sample request and learning who wrote what from back in the day.

"Make U Wet" was a hot mid to up tempo song on which Chauncey Black sang the leads while Knowledge the Pirate raps a verse. This song is sassy and a little suggestive with a nice groove and Aqil from W-N-E chanting "all night long I can make you wet" while Teddy blends the vocorder beautifully with the background vocals. This song should have gotten more of a push as it was one of the stronger songs on the album.

The track 'Booti Call" was another song Teddy started out on leads and which borrowed a familiar melody from a past mega hit. Ted starts his vocals out borrowing from the melody of the tune "Lowdown" by 70's singer Boggs Scaggs. The song played off of Bill Belamy's joke about a late night phone call from a girl being considered a "booti call". Antoine Dickey of the Pirates did his thing on the rap break. This is probably one of his best verses as a rapper in my opinion, the flow was good and it wasn't gimmicky.

One thing I loved about the creative process was that Teddy was open to allowing other producers to contribute. This song had about 10 different remixes. There were versions by Sprague, Mucho and other in house producers.

"Loves In Need" is a cover of Stevie Wonder's hit song. On the Blackstreet version Chauncey Black sings leads and the other guys all blends heavy background harmonies. I remember being there for the entire process of this song too…witnessing every drum sound being tweaked to become custom, loading sounds and take after take of vocals…whew…the end result is a beautiful rendition of a classic song.

That mega smash 'Joy" is one of Blackstreet's most notable hits. Levi Little carried this song on his back singing the leads with perfect intonation. Joy was a song partially written by Michael Jackson, Teddy Riley and Tammy Lucas.

The studio was always in lockdown stealth mode whenever Michael Jackson was in town. Levi somewhat channeled Michael's tone and implanted it into the soul of this son.

The next super standout of the first album was the hit song 'Before I Let You Go" led by Dave Holister. Dave made this a Blackstreet standard in fact, I would say he made this is now his song. Leon Sylvers contributed his production talents to this song and I can remember hearing it before any vocals were added and saying to myself this is going to be a hit.

I sat in the A Room in a lot of sessions. When Dave recorded his vocal on this song and he nailed it in just a few takes.

"Falling in Love Again" was a song that Dave Hollister sang lead vocals on. This song was a love song but not one of my favorites from the album. I can't even recall where I was when this track was being recorded.

"Tonights the Night" Tammy Lucas Chad and Pharell Williams of the Neptunes penned a classic duet where Chauncey and Tammy played off each other beautifully. Craig Mack and SWV were on the remix.

The song "Happy Home" was a sexy jazzy smooth song intended to be a power ballad. Chauncey Black sang leads on this track. This song shows Teddy's sophisticated style of production, it takes you back to a jazzy big band era with a beautiful jazz break taking place during the bridge. This is another song that had single potential, but is definitely an album classic.

The song "Wanna Make Love" took a big bite out of Roger Troutman's and Zap's hit song "Computer Love" from the opening note, to the vocorder, even the opening vocal note sounds like "Computer Love". This is when I learned the difference between clearing a sample and an interpolation of a song. Part of what I did was send clearance paperwork in to publishing companies to get the proper permission to use all of the "familiar melodies' intertwined in the creation of this album.

Dave Holister swags his way through this song but nothing special jumps out other than the fact that it sounds like "Computer Love" but Dave Holister as great as he is isn't Charlie Wilson.

'Giving You All My Lovin" starts with the familiar melody from a hit Earth Wind and Fire and ends up being a hidden jewel of the album. It's a classic

New Jack swing song that rocks so hard.

Chauncey Black did a great job leading these uptempo songs on the first Blackstreet album. Teddy and his production force held down the music and Dave and Levi carried the hits slow songs through the finish line.

I had the list of all of the album's contributors ready to be submitted for the album credit liner, but somehow a lot of names and contributions were left off including my own. Nonetheless Blackstreet's first album was finished and before it even made an official debut the buzz surrounding the album was incredible.

Part of the hype surrounding the debut of the album was due to the success of the song "Baby Be Mine" from the CB-4 Soundtrack which featured Joe Stonestreet. There were a few interludes on the album as well. That was back during the time when an album was intended to flow from beginning to end, before music switched to a singles based market.

But the stand out singles from this album really stood out. Of course "Booti Call" was a dance hit reaching #3 on the U.S. Hot Dance Singles. Comedian Bill Bellamy had made the phrase popular in one of his televised comedy routines and the beat was ridiculous thanks in part to Eric Sermon the green eyed bandit. But the remixes to this song were crazy!

AHOY! What these dudes supposed to be ...Nigga we the Pirates Twan Dickey, Knowledge the Pirate along with Harlem born Nutta Butta rapped over a series of remixes. Every in house producer got a shot to keep this song hot.

"Before I Let Go" became the stand out of the

album reaching number 7 in the U.S. Hot 100 and number 2 on the U.S. Hot R&B Single Chart. The song showcased Dave Holister as the lead vocalist and Dave took full advantage of the opportunity to make this song great. I think he channeled Donny Hathaway because Dave put that "UMPH" on the song. Teddy and I developed the concept for the video as well as the concept for the album cover art. He would dictate what he wanted in the video and we would expound on the idea until we came up with the concept.

Then I worked with talent agents to book actor Omar Epps who was still riding the fame wave from his movie "Juice" and Donna Roberts (Teddy's live in girlfriend) best friend just happen to be actress Shari Headly who EVERYBODY knew as "Lisa McDowell" in in Eddie Murphy's hit "Coming To America". We rented a Brownstone in

NY and started filming.

Teddy's oldest daughter Deja played Shari as a child in the video. Kareen styled the group in beautiful butter soft leather jackets with fad fashion head gear and a sure fire hit was created. Levi Little sang the lead on the Michael Jackson inspired hit "JOY".

I can recall the day we cut Levi's vocal for "Joy" and he hit this high note that sounded like a damn whistle. "Yo Lee how in the world did you get your voice to go that high?" I asked …"Ancient Chinese Secret TB" Levi replied jokingly. Levi was one of the original members of the group Levi was a cool guy from New Jersey up in Patterson he and Chauncey grew up together. I don't know how he came to be in the group, but he was one of the original members and he was there when I arrived but by the next album he too would be replaced.

After Levi's was replaced he and I continued to maintain communication between each other. He was a talented writer, singer, producer and musician himself and sought out to launch his own solo after leaving the group...He built a studio in Virginia Beach and from time to time I would go over there to work on projects with him. There were a lot of people who made contributions who went uncredited on the album liner credits including myself, but not getting an album credit was the least of the problems people were having. Everybody thought they should be getting, felt entitled to or expected more money!

Chapter 10

Tour Time

The album was done and it was time to start hitting the road to promote the records. Because of my position as Studio manager I didn't get a chance to go on tour with the group much but I did go out on a couple of dates with them. But before the tour there were rehearsals and Teddy brought in the best tour musicians in the business.

(Sprague Williams & Bernard Belle)

Guys he had on the road with him during the GUY days. There was Bernard Belle on Bass, the brother of R&B singer Regina Belle, Gerald Heyward was the drummer, Lauren Dawson and

Kern were two of the keyboard players. I was always impressed with musicians more than producers. I befriended all of the band members, but got along with some more than others. Lauren and Gerald were the coolest of the crew. Bernard was, dare I say.. the most talented but, he had a streak of ass-hole in him.

On a few occasions I threatened to break his fingers so he couldn't play any more probably for getting too mouthy, but overall he was cool. It was only when people like that got too uppity or got to feeling themself that I would carry a situation like that. About 20 something years later through a newly formed relationship with my father, I discovered that Bernard was actually my blood relative. I heard that he had a stroke and reached out to him as a token of peace, but Bernard for whatever reason doesn't rock with me and thats cool. I wish him well.

Dancers were also brought in and a whole new element of madness insured. "Oh they claiming these bitches" I thought to myself as the dancers were literally made "off limits" There was Michelle, Katrina, Chyna, Karima and a 4th girl who was rotated in and out. Darren Henson was brought in as a choreographer and we secured a dance studio on Bonney Road for dance rehearsals.

From the outside looking in, it would appear that there was a dancer for each of the guys in the group, but that wasn't the case. To me it seemed like all of them were Teddy's girls. So the dancers were put up in apartments around the City of Virginia and the band members stayed in one of the rental houses Teddy had.

There was also the Boggs House, a three story

townhouse on Boggs Ave which affectionately became known as "the Player's Palace". I had a room on the 3rd floor of the palace and guest producers like Will Skylz and Lil Chris Smith would stay on the second floor when they came into town to work. There were so many women in and out of that house it was ridiculous.

We had a few locations setup for the band to rehearse but Hampton University allowed us to rent their auditorium for a series of tour rehearsals and the accommodations were ideal. The stage was large enough and the sound was adequate plus the feedback from all of the college girls on campus was a good indication that this was going to be a great tour.

The guys would go out with acts such as Boyz 2 Men, New Edition, Keith Sweat, SWV, Joedci, Mary J Blige or whoever was hot at the time.

I went out with the group on tour dates that were within driving distance of Virginia Beach. Places like the Richmond Coliseum in Richmond Virginia, about 100 miles away, the Hampton Coliseum, and Raleigh North Carolina. I recall one particularly huge show in North Carolina where every major R&B act was performing. I was standing on the side of the stage with Dave Hollister watching one of the opening acts perform …."Damn I got butterflies Tone" Dave said to me "look at all them damn people man"…" you'll be good" I reassured him "y'all been practicing your ass off".

As the house lights went dim to get ready for the next act which was to be Blackstreet, Dave pulled out a small flask of liquor, took a hit and told me to hold it for him while he was on stage. He went on to tear the house down that night, Tim and I finished what was in his flask.

Teddy was a perfectionist and the Blackstreet band and sound shut everybody down. Especially Gerald Heyward, that boy was a BEAST on the drums. His power, timing and fills made me not want to touch a drum stick.

The keyboards were lush and vibrant bass was thick and chunky and the vocals were optimal thanks to sound tech Sprague "Doogie" Williams, Sprague is a multi talented guy. He has a tech side which is as equally as strong as his creative side and kept the vocals and sound intact. Other people who were instrumental in pulling off these great live performances were guys like Tim Miller, Bongo and Butch These were the RODIES and we all know roadies rock.

Tim Miller was the top roadie, a stumpy white guy with an Irish accent who only ate brown food. We would love to go hang out between rehearsals or shows with Tim because he was the type of guy who would blow a whole check on some bullshit and treat everyone who was with him.

Bongo was a hippie type guy, very slim and gaunt with scant facial hair. He was a rigger and would climb the rafters to fly speakers from the ceiling. Butch Harrison, was the black guy roadie. Butch was very smart, he had a perm and reminded me of Sly Stone. But these guys knew their craft just as well as any of the musicians or performers and were crucial to Blackstreet pulling of great shows. After the show, we were all backstage in celebratory mode when someone notified me that our keyboard player Loren Dawson was missing. "Where the Fuck was Lauren" Sifu asked. Sifu was Teddy's personal bodyguard and couldn't watch everyone.

We had additional security like Big Dave and Wayne but they were more a show of force because they were big and physically intimidating but Sifu was 5'8 of pure danger yet he wasn't about to leave Teddy's side to look for Loren.

I found out that he left with two girls. They had driven him away from the stadium into town and apparently had intentions of setting him for a robbery. I was able to locate where he was and get to him before anything bad happened but the lesson was learned …we come together and we leave together.

The group was great with Dave. I had never seen a live performance with Joe and since the group was still relatively new nobody missed Joe in live performances. Teddy was the big name that drew the crowd out initially, but eventually the songs would win fans and Chauncey Dave and Levi's individual identities began to emerge.

Blackstreet went on to do a series of successful concert and television appearances and unfortunately because I was the studio manager and not the road manager I couldn't do the European, Canadian or West Coast show dates.

I went to award shows like the Soul Train and BET Awards with the group when the opportunity presented itself, but for the most part I stayed back at the studio. Teddy tapped Tim Smith to take on the responsibility of being a road manager.

While the group was on tour it was business as usual back at the studio. But business at the studio sometime had a effect on the groups touring opportunities.

Chapter 11

WHO'S COMING OUT NEXT

While Teddy was touring other artists were waiting in the wings for their chance to impress him when he returned. Everybody wanted to book studio time yet everyday Teddy would call with a different demand, He was still getting production requests from major artists and had a handful of artists in his stable.

Wreckx - N - Effect. Aqil and Markell had a huge hit with "Rump Shaker" yet the follow up singles never rose to the same level. They were itching to get back in the studio. I think Aqil's tolerance and patience ran out, because one day I went to work and the life sized cardboard cutout of Teddy Riley had BE-HEADED by Aq wielding a sword. "Damn" it was probably one of my martial arts swords I had around the studio.

I never interfered or intervened between Teddy and Aqil or Teddy and Markell because they were brothers and their bond was more solidified than any bond I would create with either of them.

8th Ave

Singer Tyee Thurman and of the group "Blackgirl" was put with singer/songwriter LaMenga Kafi, a girl named Jazz and Beverly Johnson to form the female equivalent to

Blackstreet called 8th Ave. This was a great idea but too bad it never worked out. Having 4 bombshells hanging around the studio invited a lot of attention.

Something about Tyvee and LaMenga oozed sexiness, and I had to remind myself on a few occasions to stop flirting with these women before I ended up in the unemployment line. I did not interact with Jazz and Beverly that much but Tyvee and Lamenga were my girls and despite my constant flirting we became cool.

Teddy was very protective of them and minimized the number of guys who hung around them, but I was always around the studio. When other people were home asleep or out partying I'd be at the studio. There were a bunch of luxury apartments around Virginia Beach, where artist producers and dancers would be housed.

Certain individuals had their own places but others were paired together as roommates. After a while, to me it just started to seem like a concubine scenario with Teddy and a few of the females around the studio. That was one of the perks of celebrity, women flocked to him and sometimes a few of us "regular guys" benefited from the overflow.

Tammy Lucas

Tammy Lucas was a tremendous writer and singer, She had recorded a SMASH with Teddy "Is It Good To You" and then wrote another banger for Blackstreet with "Tonight's The Night". Tammy also wrote on Michael Jackson's "Joy" and "Remember the Time". I was certain that she would be a priority but one day I just stopped seeing her around. She was a dedicated worker and wasn't one of the people who just hung around for the hell of it.

I loved Tammy's version of Tonight's The Night but one day I heard Coko from SWV singing Tammy's part on the song. I must have blinked and missed something because I don't even know how that came about. I met the ladies of SWV when they came into Future Recording Studios to work.

Mucho and a group of guys were being immature and rude and I did not tolerate people insulting our guest. Mucho has been bothering Coko so much , joking her nails that it stressed her out and she began to cry. "Yo Mucho leave that girl along why you always fucking with somebody" I said angrily as I offered her some consolation.

Coko was a sweetheart and hell of a singer, I didn't want her energy ruined by Mucho being an asshole. I walked her inside and let her chill in my office until she got ready to record. Mucho didn't mean any harm, everybody had jokes around there and he probably wanted to interact with her differently but did not have the right approach... who knows? What I do know is that Coko replacing Tammy Lucas on that song was just another example of human indispensability based on someone's opinion.

The Pirates

The Pirates were a group of rappers who used being...well pirates as a marketing gimmick to stand out. They were two guys with dreadlocks who rapped. Knowledge rapped in almost a Das EfX style fast and choppy and his voice was unique in sound and raspy tone.

To me, Twain was mediocre as an emcee and I probably only say that because ...shit it's true I didn't like his rap style and false patois "Jafaking" accent, but he happened to be in the right place at the right time and gifted enough to pen a few verses on remixes here and there. Twain even landed a movie role playing a Jamaican. I saw him talking bout "Tick Tock Gun Shot" and was like where the fuck is that $1000 from the work I fronted you?? Of course those incident occurred way after we both left Future but in mentioning him I just wanted to add that. Pirates would set it off with out hesitation.

We were out partying at Mr. Magic's nightclub once and I look up to see Knowledge standing on the bar throwing glasses at people. The place erupted. Sifu rushed Teddy outside as gunshots started to ring out. I run out with my girlfriend Patrice gun in hand and Teddy's cousin Christo pops up from behind my car holding a shotgun..."Yo Yo Yo chill nigga its me" I said to

Christo. A few seconds later police would swarm the parking lot. Mr. Magic was a nightclub owned by an Indian guy named Ray Patel. Ray made sure we had the TOP LEVEL VIP every time we went to his club and the haters hated it. One night Sifu got into it with one of those haters and a few of his friends...before any of us could get up to help him Sifu had thrown one guy through the plate glass window, jumped through the window behind him and beat him and his buddies asses.

Chance MC was another cat that was around Future Recording Studios and by far one of the most unique rappers who came through. He hung out with the Pirates, because they shared similar styles, but Chance was a bit of a standout out with his style. Chance was an MC ahead of his time and his word play was incredible.

Nutta Butta was with the Harlem boys and had been a featured MC who was down with Wreckx-N-Effect and Blackstreet. Butta was just that smooth, He had swag before people started using the word. I thought Nutta Butta would be a solo artist along the lines of LL Cool J, to me he had that type of star power.

Nutta was never directly involved with any of the drama associated with Posse Deep or the Georgia Boys. He was just a fly MC who stood in the wings like so many artists who were around Future waiting for his shot.

When my friend boxing legend Pernell "Sweet Pea" Whitaker passed away in 2018 Nutta Butta returned to Virginia to perform at a special memorial the city of Norfolk hosted. Nutta Butta whose real name is Menton Smith is till this day a great friend and from time to time we stay in touch.

The Clipse, Initially The Clipse were intimidating to some of the people at Future recording studios and as a result they didn't want them around. The Thornton Brothers, Gene and Terrence also known as Malice and Pusha T were two guys from New York who grew up in Norfolk and were deeply hood affiliated. "Tony don't let them guys up in the studio man they be hanging around gangsters and Hustlers they bad news" I used to get warned about them but I used to also say " they are also good rappers" and try to vouch for them.

They were down with the Neptunes, Chad Shay and Pharrell and at times Teddy didn't even want THEM around, so you know when the Clipse came by it was like "tell them I'm not here" or he'd make up some excuse not to fuck with them. Busy is busy, regardless if it's producing a hit, or trying to beat the high score on Ms Pac Man machine. "he's busy" is the response they got most of the time.

Funny shit is it wasn't until after Pharrell Chad and the Neptunes really got on and started making hits that Teddy really became cool with them. It was 2019 at Pharrell's Something in the Water Event in Virginia Beach when I metaphorically saw Teddy Riley kiss Pharrell Williams ass.

He made this elaborate speech about knowing Pharrell when he was in high school and they made nice for the audience. "Can you believe this phoney ass shit right here?" I was standing beside a few other people who worked at the studio and we looked at each other and the same thought had to have been in our minds..." listen to this bullshit". Back in 92 it was a different story, Teddy didn't care much for Pharrell back then, did he forget the times he talked shit about this dude?

Nonetheless bygones are bygone. I even had dinner with Teddy that evening after all the shit we had been through but back to the story.

Troy Mitchell I had a friend of mine who was really more like a little brother. He lived across the street from me growing up in the same neighborhood and I had known him even before I went into the army. Troy Mitchell who had been in the group 3 Feet when they were signed to London Polygram Records. Troy along with 3 Feet had been on Salt and Pepper's hit "What a Man" and had an entire album completed before getting dropped from his deal with London Polygram so I was trying to hook him up with Teddy because both Teddy and Markel had recently acquired new labels.

Teddy had L.O.R Records label and Markell had Funky Mama Records I introduced them. Now since I first showed him how to work a keyboard and after having worked with Hurby Azor and DJ Wiz from Kid and Play Troy had developed into a dope producer. He was very good at sampling (which at the time was extremely tedious) and creating beats which requires a lot of creativity and soul. Troy played some music for Teddy and Teddy was very impressed but Troy emphasized to him that he'd made that music at another producer studio and didn't have equipment of his own.

So Teddy gave me the green light to buy Troy a keyboard. I went to Audio Light & Musical and met up with my favorite sales rep for hippie looking dude named Robbie to buy Troy an Ensoniq EPS keyboard and Teddy was supposed to bring him on board as one of the staff producers, but in addition to being one of the illest producers in Virginia Troy was also one of the illest MCs at the time in the Nation. I told him before he came on board that "this Teddy train moves kind of slow and sometimes in funny directions bro. You and I are closer than that and I don't want you to come into this situation and end up hurting this man because you don't get what you expect."

Instead Troy ended up linking up with Timbaland who was just getting his career started and found a place on Timbaland's first three albums being featured as an MC. Teddy never asked me to go get a keyboard from Troy LMAO ...he knew what the end result would be.

Queen Pen I'd say from 1991 through 1998 the only artist that successfully released an entire album through Teddy or Markell's labels was my girl Lynese Walter aka Queen Pen. Queen Pen's release had more to do with death threats than Teddy's personal willingness to put her out. Queen Pen and were what I would consider very close platonic friends at that time.

We hung out together whenever she wasn't recording mostly smoking trees and eating in front of the fireplace at her condo.

I was messing with a girl from Hampton University who I used to sometimes bring around the studio. Dee Dee was a tall slender shapely girl from Queens who favored Aalyiah.

She was bi-curious and whenever I would bring her around the studio QueenPen used to always say how pretty she was. I told Dee Dee and she got excited...I didn't *think* Lynese was gay, but she had a phat gorgeous ass and girls would always comment on her shape. Plus, she had that beautiful complexion and facial features and was so down to earth everybody loved her.

I arranged for them to hang out thinking some sexy shit was about to jump off and I'd be the middle man so to say, but I wasn't invited. Dammit Lyncsc! I picked Dee Dee up a few hours later and discovered that all they did was drink, talk and do girly shit. Queen Pen was about her business and was always ready to record. She stayed in the studio late nights, wrapped up in a blanket writing raps, sipping tea, determined to get her time in and album done... She spent a lot of time waiting for Teddy...waiting for him to finish shooting pool or playing video games in the rec room, or finish up a session with another artist so one of the engineers can put her track on and she can get in the booth.

Once Queen Pen's album was finished, everyone was excited to get to the next phase, shooting videos, writing releases and one sheets doing all of the marketing and promotional work it took to make a song a success. She had other female artists that could have been considered competition like Lil Kim, Foxy Brown E.V.E but I saw Lynese initially approach these women from a sisterly point of view having no animosity or beef with any other female artists. Queen Pen kept it G. But if they came for her she let them have it.

During that time, a new technology had emerged called "Enhanced CDs" where if a fan purchased an "Enhanced CD" and put it inside of a computer extra information about the artist with pop up.

Teddy brought the software which was called Macromedia Director and that software allowed me to make enhanced CDs for the Queen Pen project... Teddy wanted me to learn the software and teach it to him. So, every chance I got, I would make something for the enhanced CD then show Teddy how I made it. Deep inside, the geek in him ate that shit up, but he was inundated with production tasks and was too busy to really get into computers for anything other than music.

The Queen Pen album was done, the enhanced CD was done, all of the artwork finished and the marketing plan was in place but the release date was not set. The release date for Queen Pen's album was delayed so many times she sought help from some gangsters in New York to lean on Teddy and get her album out. Threats started coming in and apparently Teddy pulled whatever strings he needed to to get Queen Pen's album to the public.

Those New York cats were not fucking around with Teddy over Queen Pen's album and they were credible. That was a time when we started wearing bulletproof vests to work. Imagine working in a creative environment like a recording studio where love songs and beautiful music is being made, but having to wear a bulletproof vest to work.

Studios are creative environments but greedy, seedy people can turn any place into a violent atmosphere, Tupac was shot in a recording studio, so was Jam Master Jay and later even Omar

Chandler who was the first person I met at Future Recording Studio, would lose his life in a studio. It's not supposed to come with the territory, but unfortunately it does and I knew for a fact that if they ever came for Teddy they'd try to get me and Sifu out of the way first. Sifu was Teddy's personal bodyguard, a dangerous martial artist who was known to go hard for Teddy and I had a reputation outside of the studio and was trained by the military to kill. I didn't fuck around.

Men Of Vision Every species is territorial especially men with a lot of testosterone flowing through their system...shit can get out of hand sometimes. This was the case with Men Of Vision. Men of Vision was Michael Jackson's group and came to Virginia to work on their debut album. That this is a era where they were a few male R&B groups out. You had Boys to Men, New

Edition, Jodeci, H-Town, Silk, Shai...the list goes on, but Spanky Williams Desmond Gregg, Brian Deramius and Corely Randolph were a young hot upcoming R&B group backed by the King of Pop himself.

A bunch of fucking pretty boys...even Spanky, the chubby one could pull your girl. So it was no big surprise to me when another rooster stepped into Teddy's hen house. I mean with him always away on the road and having to divide his time between all the other chicks like the dancers, the members of the girl groups, female assistants, interns and the like it was only a matter of time before a smooth criminal would steal some goodies from his main chick.

The guys in M.O.V were as cool as any of the guys in Blackstreet. Spanky was a fantastic musician and vocalist. They worked very smoothly in the studio and differently from Blackstreet. They had a hit with the single "Housekeeper" a song Ted co-wrote. Little did he know that one of those guys would be keeping house with his old lady. It was a big stink and led to a bunch of bullshit. Somebody from their organization, I believe it was their manager J.R., stabbed Teddy's car tires in the studio parking lot one day. Teddy's cousin Chris Washington who we called "Christo" and I got armed and we drove over to where Men of Vision were staying.

We blocked the entire cul-de-sac and marched down Boggs St. like a posse of cowboys in a western movie calling them out. I thought to myself as we walked down the street "This is some bullshit..one man cuts another man's car tires because another man is fucking that man's girlfriend and we're the ones out here with guns..." That's the kind of blind loyalty I had at the time. To me it was more than a job by now, this is family we melded together, so if you mess with one of us you mess with all of us. Their manager, J.R. came outside with a few guys from the group. One of them, Brian came out of the house with what looked like a .38 but we had shotguns uzi's tech nines glocks and they knew they were outnumbered.

Christo and I ended up arranging a meeting with Teddy and their manager to hash things out and put an end to this issue before things got out of hand.

I set up the meeting to take place at a Ruby Tuesday's restaurant about four blocks away from the studio. I called in a bunch of young gangsters from Portsmouth who would shoot a motherfucker just for studio time and had the whole place surrounded with shooters just in case something went south. We had a lot of official gangsters who knew Teddy. East coast niggas west coast nigga Bloods Crips and these guys had hitters at the ready. They would always try extorting Teddy for discounted beats or musical favors and as silly as it sounds I felt as if I always had to be on point so I stayed armed.

My Military training had taught me more ways to kill a man than I care to remember, my bro Troy was a street general and had a team of young soldiers who were ready too. Fortunately everyone came out of Ruby Tuesday's and the beef was squashed but, my people were kind of upset that they didn't get any action.

Chapter 12

Sore From The Tour

Back on tour, the 1st album was booming and fans were very responsive to the group. Blackstreet was by all means a new R&B act out touring with New Edition, Joedci and Boyz II Men. But the secret weapon was Teddy Riley's maniacal drive for perfection and that band that he put together. That band was fire! As an opening act they made it hard to follow them and as a headliner they never disappointed. The television promotional circuit took them to all of the late night talk show programs, award show appearances and such. The actual tour took them all across the United States as well as to Europe and to Japan.

Teddy didn't join Blackstreet on some of the overseas dates and Japan dates because he was back in Virginia producing Michael Jackson but whenever the group was on the road there was a sense of peace at the studio. All of the people who just hung around to kiss Teddy's ass faded away until he came back into town and all of the producers and writers who were serious about their craft booked session time.

But It was also when Teddy was on the road that the other studio employees thought they could get away with fucking off...NOT ON MY WATCH. I made sure people did what it was they were supposed to do. I learned leadership early in the military. I was the youngest squad leader on the Special Reaction Team and leading a squad of rangers prepped me for anything, especially these jokers at the studio. I wouldn't threaten to fire them, but I'd promise to beat their ass into compliance if they tried to play me I'd take it personal.

"You know Teddy put me in charge while he is gone. If you don't do what is supposed to be done on my watch, how does that reflect on me?" There was an incident once when Earl, Teddy's personal assistant didn't go out of town with Teddy and the group and was hanging around the studio.

Without my knowledge Earl took the studio van and drove to downtown Norfolk. While Earl was out cruising at 3am he had an accident with a lady delivering newspapers and hauled ass. He committed a hit and run in a big ass van that had "FUTURE RECORDING STUDIOS" plastered on both sides and the back. Earl parks the van back at the studio and disappears.

The lady arrives at the studio demanding $500,000 because Teddy Riley (not Earl Thomas) crashed into her 12 year old station wagon and cracked the rear light lens. I was able to resolve the situation with a lot of apologizing, $300 cash, a quick studio tour, some fake autographed Wreckx-N-Effect merchandise and an empty promise to let Teddy hear her daughter sing once he got back to Virginia, but I let Earl have it!

My reputation was somewhere between enforcer and protector... nobody is going to do anything to us but we have to do what we must. It was a demand for mutual respect. Aint going to be no mice playing while the cats are away.

By 1995 Levi had left the group, bottom line the issue was money on Levi's part. Levi felt as if the money was not being split fairly and spoke up about it but Teddy would have you believe it was his choice to put Levi out. He talked about Levi's showmanship, particularly after one concert where Levi went THEE fuck in on "Joy".

Joy was a beautiful ballad written by Michael Jackson, Tammy Lucas and Teddy Riley. "Joy" didn't make the Michael Dangerous album however, the song was perfect for Blackstreet. Levi of course sang lead on Joy and in this one particular show Levi took the audience to church towards the end of the song and unexpectedly extended the arrangement and started screaming "Joy' Joy Joy" and running back and forth across the stage. I remember standing in the wings and seeing Teddy's expression. It was a look as if to say "what in the hell is he doing?"

After Levi left the group he and I kept in touch for years to come. Levi, like so many others who came to Future Records, made Virginia his home. Levi eventually went solo, building his own studio in Virginia Beach and started working with other Virginia artists such as Bruce Hornsby.

Dave left around the same time as Levi. After coming in to replace Joe Stonestreet, Dave himself was soon gone. A great part of the success of the first Blackstreet album was due to the phenomenal take off of "Before I Let You Go" which Dave sang lead vocal on.

I had heard the track progress from the very first beat Teddy laid down in the A-Room until the moment Dave stepped out of the booth and knew instantly that song was going to be a difference maker. Chauncey had attempted the leads on the song before Dave but Dave's vocals worked best.

Maybe the success of "Joy" and "Before I Let Go" sparked some envy on Chauncey Black's behalf. Chauncey had the leads on over half of the song on the album. But the 2 standout singles were definitely "Joy" which Levi led and "Before I Let You Go" which of course Dave led. It's possible that the success of these songs led both Levi and Dave to think that solo success would be inevitable. You know their heads got big-heads and their egos took over, It's also quite possible that the response from the fans when these songs were performed live led to internal envy. It seemed as if Chauncey got a little jealous of the shine Levi and Dave received. I could see it in the effort he put into his performances. At rehearsals Chauncey went hard, I saw his confidence as a performer grow.

Black seemed to have had the mentality that if he couldn't get the response from the crowd that Dave and Levi got from singing their songs he'd drive them crazy another way… he'd take his shirt.

So Black would rip open his shirt to expose his chiseled six pack to the women and it worked for him. Girls would show up at the studio and wait for Chauncey…FOR HOURS…

Dave on the other hand was sneaky with it. It would be nothing to go by one of the dancers' houses and see Dave creeping out. Dave Hollister was definitely the ladies man and nobody's girl was safe. He even tried to smash my second wife.

I think it was the magical gift of the mouth…Dave's vocal intensity and prowess created weak spots in these women's armor and they gave in but, there was one woman he met who would reverse that.

A sexy light skinned thick thing from Portsmouth I think she even inspired one of his solo hits "Baby Momma Drama". The night they met Tim Smith, Lil Chris, Dave and I were on our way to Columbus Station Condos where Lee "Big Bubb" Drakeford lead singer from the group "Today" was staying. Big Bubb was a hell of a singer and first class fool meaning he had a great sense of humor. Back during this time Bubb was also a stone-cold FREAK!

Bubb used to stay on the prowl, but this night he was hosting a strip party at his house. I was cool with a lot of exotic dancers chicks through one I was close with named Karamel and used to get strippers from the local strip clubs for parties and VIP events. I hit Karamel up and she had a stable of bad bitches on speed dial. Bubb was in full party mode as we arrived and we were greeted at the door by him dressed in a silk bathrobe, like the Black Huge Heffner, true player style. Bubb opened the door threw his arms up in the air and said "Come On In And Get Your Dick Sucked!" we walked in to a strip party....Dave walked out with a fiancee'. Well, she wasn't instantly his fiancee, but she did end up becoming his wife.

More and more we'd see the fine light skinned chick from P-Town hanging around the studio until it was finally official. She made it to a "main chick" event. What's a main chick event? That's a private more family oriented affair where no dancers or girl group members were allowed, no female assistants or interns… just the safe girls the ones NOBODY wanted to mess with.

We'd be at these type of scenarios and there would be Chauncey, Teddy and Levi with their main girls who all got along with each other to a degree and now Dave was bringing the girl he'd met at the strip party to the main girl events…"Yo aint that the girl from Bubb's house?" Yep that's all Dave's now. You see between tour dates and appearances the group would return to Virginia and relax. These were fun times they came back enthusiastic and gratified with the success they were receiving from adoring fans across the country.

In Virginia, Blackstreet, Teddy Riley and Wreckx-N-Effect were the hometown heroes. After the first set of tour dates Teddy was pumped and production requests were coming in left and right and not only that, Aarron Hall and Damion Hall from Teddy's old group GUY started coming around more and more and talks of another album began. "Damn Teddy going to be in Guy Wreckx-N-Effect and Blackstreet" I wonder how that's gonna work out.

Aaron's presence intimidated the guys in Blackstreet, nobody would say anything but they respected Aaron and the dynamics of he and Teddy's relationship was difficult to explain. One minute they were cool and acting like besties and the next minute they were doing interviews dissing each other.

The excessive number of production requests created a problem when it came to Teddy making all of the tour dates, especially when he had Michael Jackson stuff to do. Missing a concert date because you have to produce a Michael

Jackson song is an understandable priority, but these absences from certain dates, especially the Japan dates gave Levi, Dave and Chauncey something to gripe about.

From my understanding the European dates without Teddy were more fun to the group, because apparently things got lackadaisical when Teddy wasn't around and no Teddy meant they can split the money 3 ways now and if they omitted the band and performed to a track instead their pockets would get even fatter.

You see its my belief that Levi and Dave put that type of shit in Chauncey's ear while Teddy was absent, but Chauncey had more loyalty to Teddy and came back to let him know what the other guys were up to. "How the fuck does Teddy know what we were planning? Wasn't nobody around but me you and punk ass Chauncey" I heard Dave saying to Levi. I just started laughing because Dave was right. Chauncey spilled the beans.

Dave had done a lot of recording before joining Blackstreet. He recorded songs with Tupac like "Brenda Had a Baby" and "Keep Your Head Up" and worked with Jodeci to name a few. So Dave's ambition to record his own stuff after joining the group didn't go away, but Teddy wasn't with it, sprinkle that with the girls Dave hit around the studio that Teddy either had too or wanted PLUS the shit that Chauncey was going back telling Teddy, then add a demand for more money as the cherry on top and you got a Dave Hollister split.

Dave became a successful solo artist after leaving Blackstreet. His first album "Ghetto Hymns" had a few hot songs like "Favorite Girl" and "Baby Momma Drama" nothing that would ever chart higher than "Before I Let Go" but songs that sustained his career and solidified him as a solo artist. Not every standout singer that leaves a group scenario is able to parlay their talents into a successful solo career. That's the lightning in a bottle phenomena that hit people like Michael Jackson, Lionel Ritchie, Bobby Brown and Justin Timberlake...it didn't quit hit Dave and Levi like that.

Chapter 13

Downtime

Around 1994 Teddy decided he wanted to renovate the entire studio around a new studio console he was getting. The console in a recording studio is the centerpiece of the facility and a producer of Teddy's caliper and a recording studio called Future had to have the latest gear. We had a state of the art SSL and Neve Consoles in the A-

Room and B-Room. Before renovation the studio looked like a morgue.

The A room had been a dark shade of purple with black accents and multi color sound diffusers placed about the walls. There was a game room to the left of the front entrance with all sorts of stand alone vintage arcade games like Ms Pac Man, Galaga, Space Invaders and a huge pool table. Down the hallway past the game room on the left was a small kitchen area and Teddy's personal bathroom and the public bathroom.

Teddy's personal bathroom was more like a walk in closet with a small twin size bunk bed and private bathroom in it. The first door on the right led to the "A-Room", the main recording area at Future Recording Studios.

Walking through the double sound proof doors into the A-Room and turning left you would see

Teddy's producer's console loaded with drum machines, samplers and keyboards. Just ahead of that was the equipment counter which held all of the outboard gear and in front of that was the studio console.

On the far left of the A-Room was the tape room, a small closet that was converted into another one of Teddy's private bedrooms and one of the entrances to the vocal booth. To the very front of the studio was the LIVE ROOM, a huge space which could accommodate a full band but was mostly being used for storage.

The Live room had a rollup garage style door we used to load gear in and out and the second entrance to the vocal booth.

The B-Room was a smaller pre-production studio at the end of the hallway where the ideas of junior producers were born, The rental rate on the B

Room was much less than the A-room but booth rooms sounded great. The B Room was very unorganized and junky when I first arrived but during the renovation process I made sure to equip the B Room with the same outboard gear the A-Room had.

With the exception of the 2 inch tape machine, the mixing console and the size, the rooms were pretty much identical. Of course all of the engineers wanted to work in the A-Room but producers like David Wynn, Mucho Scott, Will Skillz Stewart and Lil Chris didn't mind working in the B-Room.

Next to the B-Room was my office. I kept my area neat and tidy. Every invoice, sample clearance form, production split agreement, insurance document and equipment inventory tucked neatly away in a file cabinet and backed up on floppy disks which, I kept off site at home in case something happened to the original. In addition to managing the studio I helped prepare the paperwork required to clear samples and I processed writers' splits for publishing documents so I had a lot of files.

I was meticulous and paid attention to detail. Future Recording Studio was a popular studio facility but it wasn't the best studio. There was a local guy named Rob Ulsh who owned Master Sound Recording Studio. Rob and I became great friends after I brought his first 2 industry projects to his studio. Soon Timbaland would book blocks at Master Sound to produce his early hits with Aalyiah Missy and Ginuwine.

Prior to that I had DJ Wiz from Kid and Play in Master Sound working on music for local artists 3 Feet. After acquiring designs from Studio

Banton, I hired a local contractor from Chesapeake named Herby Hawks, owner of Hawks Construction Company, to complete the plans according to design.

We threw in some extra fly shit like a lighted glass receptionist desk, with black granite counter tops, black marble floors and plasma flat screen TVs in the foyer.

The ugly purple was replaced by an elegant silver and black theme with silver textured walls and black marble floor to replace the worn high traffic carpet that had been there before. The game consoles were taken out in lieu of a television video game console broadcast to a movie screen from a projector.

The felt on the pool table was replace and rightfully so after the white girl receptionist got caught having sex on the pool table with a in house producer. Oddly enough Teddy sent the producer back to Cali but kept the receptionist around a little longer.

He also had a dog kennel added to the studio and a dog kennel built at his mansion. The dog kennel at the mansion came in at $20,000 and featured 3 climate control dog houses, a concrete run surrounded by gravel then grass, a PA system so that Teddy or Donna could talk to the dogs from the house.

There was also a wrought iron remote control fence that could be opened from the house. This was cool because if an intruder entered their property they could sic the dogs on them without leaving the house. Plus they had a fresh running water troff.

The kennel at the studio was more simple and along the lines of a backyard deck with matching dog houses. I had some experience working with Military police training dogs from my Army days, but I had never met anyone who could bond with and work with dogs like Aaron Hall.

Aaron had these crazy huge mastiffs that he would cross breed with rottweilers and they were trained better than any Sunday school kid. Aaron gave his dogs commands in African so no one could understand the command he gave them, unless they spoke the same language. Once he had his dog guard this guy named Rodeo who made the remark "Aaron your dogs aint all that."

 Aaron told the dog in African to watch Rodeo and the dog stood directly in front of Rodeo and would growl every time Rodeo made the slightest movement. Aaron told Rodeo "Nigga if you move this dog is going to tear your ass up" Then he turns to the rest of us and says…"C'mon y'all let's go to iHop my treat" we all left laughing at Rodeo who was afraid to move because of the dog.

After about 45 minutes or so we returned from iHop and Rodeo was still being guarded by the dog "Aaron come on man get this crazy ass dog I gotta pee" Rodeo said writhing as if he was about to piss on himself.

During these downtimes is when a lot of hustlers and scammers would pop up trying to see what or who they could come up off of. Everybody had a beeper or pager back then but the technology was changing fast, from regular beepers to 2 way pagers. I recall getting a beep from someone and having to call a number and dictate to an operator what you wanted your text to say...Crazy how things evolved so fast but none so much as the cell phone.

My man Hootie Bang was the king of the cell phone burners and would hook everybody at the studio up with Motorola Flip Phone with the chip where you would just talk until the phone died and then buy a new one. Bang would come to the studio with an olive green laundry bag filled with flip phones and his cousin Spud who worked for the cell phone company would give us unlock codes.

Even I learned how to program the phones to make them work without having a recurring bill. Everybody at the studio copped a phone from Bang to avoid paying those ridiculous cellular bills. Problem was somebody figured out how to scam folks by selling them phones that were either about to be turned off or couldn't be unlocked to reprogram.

So it became an issue of watch who you get your phone from. Bang and Spud were the plugs on the phone but Bang was also the plug on many things.

After introducing him to Keivan, they grew close and our clique got stronger, but one day I got a funny phone call from Keivan "Yo Tony Brown …yo you might have to come get me ..this nigga bang is crazy and I'm about to get out the car and leave" Keivan said nervously over his burner phone. "Whats going on" I asked " I dont know he pulled up to some projects out somewhere called Newport News gave me a gun and a whole bag full of guns and told me to wait right here" Keivan said. "If he told you to wait, why you wanna leave?" I asked "Did he ask you to ride with him? "No, he said he was going to get some weed and I asked if I could go" Kevian explained. "Well you can't get out and walk from bad News back to

Virginia Beach.." I started to explain but Keivan interrupted "Wait Bad News? I said Newport News why you call it "Bad News"...."The same reason Bang gave you the gun and told you stay in the car" I said.

I could hear Bang returning to the car as we were talking and Keivan sounded a lot more relieved. Then, through the phone I heard Bang say "look at this" to which Keivan responded "DAMN We going to ride back with all of that weed" ...his voice got nervous all over again.

Bang had returned to the car with no less than 5 pounds of weed in a duffle bag. Keivan was from New York and had to learn they way we moved in Virginia, but he fell in place quick.

He was with me the night I got pulled over in my Mercedes and the police found one of Teddy's guns in my car. Teddy had used my car earlier to run to see some lady, he didnt want anyone Donna to know he was gone so he left his Porsche at the studio and asked if he could use my car.

When he got back to the studio Keivan Pookie and I left to make a run to 7-11 to grab a few things because we had chicks coming over from the Eastern Shore. As I turn into the 7-11 parking lot a Virginia Beach police officer makes a U-turn and pulls in the parking lot behind me. I go to get out of the car and as I open the door I hear him yell "GUN GUN"...He sees a black Glock 9mm on the floor between the driver's seat and door.

I hadn't even noticed Teddy's gun when I got in the car. My gun was tucked in the hidden compartment and they never found it. It was still there after I got my car back from impound. But that night I got charged with carrying a concealed weapon, Pookie got charged with possession of weed, Keivan and the Black cop knew each other from high school or some shit and they let him go.

Teddy accused Keivan of having his gun again but paid to bail me out and help me pay for a lawyer. It was ridiculous because in addition to the gun charge I was also charged with being in possession of a Narcotic. Yep narcotics.

I had been hanging with Will Skylz all day earlier and he pulled out this packet with a little label on it which said "LOVE STONES" and had a picture of a frog licking out its tongue. "Man this shit right here" Will started explaining "this shit will have your jank hard all night fam" "I looked at the package *"Love Stones, Wet stone and apply generously to penile shaft for prolonged erections"* Man what is this shit I inquired "Makes your dick stay hard" Will said it's all natural.

Okay, with these girls I had coming from the Eastern Shore tonight I wanted to be Superman Lover especially since shawty said she was bringing her girl to share with me and the rest of her friends were for Pookie, Keivan and Will...So I asked Will Skylz for one of the Love stones, which were small, hard and black irregular shaped pebbles about the size of a piece of Runts candy.

I had put it in my pocket earlier and forgotten about it. As the officer searched me he found the stone in my pocket and it seems like he was the one who got a hard on. "Aw he got that new narcotic shit" the officer said excitedly and to my surprise. "That's not a narcotic, it's all natural and sold in a package I said" "You can buy this freaky shit in New York boy but here in Virginia this is illegal" the officer responded. The substance was called "Bufotinine" and was made from Frog sweat.

How the fuck is this a narcotic in Virginia but not New York? The female judge who heard the case found it rather amusing to humiliate me by having me repeat the product directions from the packaging label.

My life may have been altered that night because Teddy wanted to go see a chick using my car and either he forgot to take his gun or as he says "Keivan took the gun and stashed it" in my car, knowing he'd be leaving with me later. I leaned more towards believing that he forgot it, nonetheless I plead "No Contest" and didn't have to do any time on any of the charges. Since then Virginia has implemented a mandatory 5 year sentence for those charges.

It was odd to me that Teddy had this huge mansion with a live-in girlfriend but little apartments and condos that he maintained with all of the side chicks. Why not just marry the mother of your children and do the right thing. He always told me that if he ever got married he would lose a lot of his female fan base....Does Donna believe this shit? I thought...I was married to my children's mother at the time.

I didn't think like that but of course I was no celebrity. Donna would invite my daughters Chiara and Danielle to come over for playdates with her daughters Deja and Taja but my own relationship was failing because, I was being accused of getting just as much ass as Teddy Riley and eventually I would get divorced from my first wife Zina, but Thanks to Teddy's busy schedule I eventually met my second wife Patrice.

Teddy was busy working in the studio with Michael Jackson and had a conflict with another event that he had scheduled. This particular night Teddy was supposed to judge the Swimsuit Model of the Year Competition sponsored by Jet Magazine but couldn't attend. I had just set up a 2inch reel in the A room where Teddy was working "Hey Tony, what are your plans for tonight?" Teddy asked. I knew better than to make plans because my beeper would go off mid way through anything I would be doing and I'd have to cut it short. "Not much whats up?" I replied. "Do you wanna take my place and be a judge in a swimsuit model competition?" Hell that was a no brainer.

I went to represent Teddy and sat on a panel of judges when I saw Patrice Ward, who had been a contestant in the contest. Aside from being one of the baddest women in the event she stood out because her voice was pretty even though she nervously forgot the words to the song she stood out.

After the competition I asked her for her number and we went out and eventually began to date. I made sure to keep her away from the vultures at the studio. Dave Hollister, Chauncey and Teddy oh Hell no my woman aint going nowhere near them niggas and I was right in feeling that way after she came to drop lunch off to me one day and Chauncey Black felt her on the ass. I semi snapped out and became very angry because at the time Patrice was more than just another girl to me this one I was serious about Chauncey was considered a brother and that was disrespectful.

After she told me I was going to hunt him down and break his fucking arm for being disrespectful but Teddy calmed me down. From that day forth I never invited any girl I dated to that studio. Girls at the studio was a commonplace thing, but it also created a very subliminally competitive environment.

The backup dancers and various girl group members were coveted. My man Keivan ruffled a few feathers by dating one of the backup dancers. A beauty named Kareema, who was a pretty ass "around the way" type girl and she was not like the other dancers in the sense that she didn't hold herself for a member of the group. A few of the other dancers were sort of gullible thinking that they belonged to the guys in the group. "I'm so and so's girl on tour" and "I'm so and so'…

Kareema was Keivan's and since Keivan wasn't a celebrity or part of the group this created a little animosity. Anytime anyone would complain about

Keivan Teddy would tell me to fire him. Now Earl Thomas, as I mentioned earlier was sort of like Teddy's personal assistant. Earl would cook, do laundry, run errands. He was super tight with Teddy's family, mother Riley, Donna and the kids. Earl even knew all of Teddy's side pieces so it was a low down dirty backstabbing move Teddy pulled on Earl when Earl introduced Maddy to Teddy.

When I first saw Maddy she was over at Earls apartment chilling on the sofa Earl was cooking and I went to pick up some food for the guys at the studio "Damn Star" I joked with Earl, you got a cute one there boy. Earl had a knack for pulling women.

He had all kinds of little tricks to trap a chick. The best one was to call the pay phone in the women's bathroom of the local night club and ask "Did anyone call Future Records for Teddy Riley or Earl?".

Once Earl introduced Maddy to Teddy it was a wrap. "Teddy took your girl Earl...Damn". I saw it coming as clear as day, women would always try to use one of us to get closer to Teddy, but Earl fell for it. Teddy took an extra liking to Maddy, it was obvious when he hired her. "Tony I'm hiring Maddy to help you" Teddy told me "I want you to show her everything she needs to know". "What? The girl from Earl's house?" I already had Tim Smith as an assistant manager and things were running well.

Maddy was not interested in learning anything from me; she had an ulterior motive and every woman who worked at Future Recording Studio knew it too. None of them liked her, even the ones that Teddy was not involved with didn't care for Maddy. I didn't care either way, I would sit down with her and try to show her how to do paperwork, how the schedules and inventories worked but her focus was elsewhere.

She was making plans showing up at the studio buck naked in noting but a trench coat. To meet Teddy.

The women who worked there smeared a lot of dirt on Maddy, because they knew Teddy would eventually start showing her the same or more attention and they were already sharing his time. Other people foresaw what was about to happen. Maddy made her way all the way in to the top dog…It was like fuck your feelings Earl, that's one of Teddy's janks now.

After I left Future Recording Studios Maddy would eventually become the HBIC "Head Bitch In Charge". She even had Teddy's baby. But let me slow down, for now I'm still in the picture and involved in everything going on at Future. I'm on phone calls with MCA reps, Interscope reps people from MJJ Productions doing song clearances with publishing companies and maintaining an employee schedule and equipment inventory.

She wasn't ready for all of that at the time. Aaron Hall told me once after I had left "Teddy's shit never ran smoother than it did when you were there, he let that bitch run shit now aint shit getting done right."

We had a lot of recreational activity that we got into at Future Recording Studios. Teddy is an avid bowler, no really, a person would be just as impressed by his bowling and pool playing as they would by his music. It was like a vagabond team of semi pro bowlers entering the alley. Everybody had their own bowling balls and shoes. Teddy was a hook bowler who could finesse the ball. I was a straight power bowler. I would try to knock the back wall down.

We went bowling all of the time at the AMC Bowling alley on Lynnhaven Parkway in Virginia Beach. Whatever celebrity who was in town during the time got caught up in the bowling frenzy. My bowling buddy was singer Cheryl Lynn who had a few post disco, pre hip hop hit songs like "To Be Real" and "Encore" It would never fail that we would be in the bowling alley and one of her songs would come on. "Oohhhhh'" shit thats my song literally."

Cheryl was very friendly and fun to be around. Another recreational pastime we did around the studio was playing basketball. We had a portable basketball hoop in the parking lot in front of the studio and everybody thought they were the next

Michael Jordan. Games would get intense between the NY crew and the Georgia crew I think the level of shit talking on the basketball court led to a few fist to cuffs but nothing too serious. The thing that pissed the guys off is when Teddy would park the Ferrari too close to the hoop and nobody could play because everyone was afraid to hit the car.

We also spent fun times in the Plaza skating rink, at the Virginia Beach boardwalk and at the oceanfront jet skiing. One recreational activity that I never ever indulged in was gambling. The studio was at times like a mini casino, Teddy and Markell would bet tens of thousands of dollars on pool games, cee-low games and cards. I didn't like losing so I didn't play plus the stakes would get high quickly.

A $50 bet could end up being a $10,000 debt.

Markell had a friend named Ralph who went by the name Rodeo. Rodeo was a small time hustler rolling around in Virginia Beach making crack plucks, trying to keep up with the Rileys. Rodeo was a bit of a showoff, but he was a cool lil dude who reminded you of Barney Rubble from the Flintstones...he would always use the term "Stick" to refer to you...as in "Whats happening Stick?". Rodeo and his cousins House and Nat would come by the studio to see Teddy and Markell just to gamble with them.

One night Teddy ran up a huge bill losing to House and didn't have the money on hand so House wanted to buck on Teddy.

Now while I liked Rodeo, I didn't like his cousin House and didn't need a reason to fuck him up fortunately, it didn't come to that, but it was known that Teddy aint getting bullied or fucked with if Tony Brown or Sifu is around. During one of these gambling occasion Puff Daddy was at Future Recording Studios gambling against Teddy and Teddy was busting his ass.

Puffy was in Virginia along with Jennifer Lopez to work on something with Teddy. He and Teddy and a few other guys were in the pool room gambling. J-Lo was sitting in the lounge area in the hallway and I was sitting in my office when Earl Thomas came to me and said in his heavy Trinidadian accent "Boy who left this money here" showing me a brown paper bag full of money, I looked in the bag and it was bout $20K "It has to be Puff's or Teddy's money I said.

Earl took the bag into the pool room and asked "Did somebody leave their money near the water cooler?" Puff looked up and once he realized that it was his money he then turned to J-Lo and proceeded to curse her the fuck out for leaving the bag of money sitting around.

Both Earl and I were surprised at how he spoke to her. "Stupid Bitch you left my shit sitting out in the open"Movies were another huge source of recreation during downtimes at the studio.

We had 2 "go to" theatres. Military Circle Mall which was the hood spot and Lynnhaven Mall which was the bougie movie theatre. Teddy was working with New Kids on The Block once and the whole group was in town to record.

While the primary vocalist were cutting vocal the rest of the guys wanted to go check out a new movie. Tim was at the studio I had some time so I decided that I would drive them there in the Studio van. We entered the theatre without any incident but before the movie was over the theatre manager came to me tapped me on the shoulder and said y'all are going to have to leave out of the back door.

A small mob of about 100 or so fans had noticed one of the guys from the group and surrounded the front of the theatre. I inconspicuously walked out, got the van and drove to the back of the theatre while the manager escorted them out of a back mall entrance. I was slightly nervous because we didn't have any security and didn't know how inconspicuous I could be in a full sized van decorated with Teddy's face logo and the words Future Recording Studios plastered across the side but we managed to get out okay. Sometimes not having a full security team was a better choice than traveling with a huge entourage besides I was a martial arts expert, ex police officer elite soldier, with a college degree in communications, if I could not diffuse a situation I was confident enough to know how to escape safely and protect who was with me.

I took Pattie Labelle to a local Food Lion grocery store because she wanted to cook for the staff at the studio. Just me and Pattie walking the isle she insisted on pushing her own shopping cart. A store employee thinks he recognizes her but he isnt really sure so he walks down each aisle we are on and acts like he is fixing items on the shelf until he finally gets the nerve to say "Did anybody ever tell you you look like Pattie Labelle?" She teased him a little by saying "You think so?"

Before we left the store the check out clerk called the stock boy up to the front of the store and said "Mr James Look it's Pattie Labelle..Mr James is your biggest fan" "Lord I thought that was you" Mr James exclaimed in a very feminine manner "Chile I have all of your tapes, that all thats in my walkman". Patti politely signed her autograph on a grocery bag and we made it safely back to the studio where she made the meanest chicken dinner for the crew.

Earl was by default the studio cook and made curry chicken and other Caribbean dishes better than any restaurant but this was Patti's time to shine. Patti actually wanted to cook to take a break from the way Teddy was driving her in the studio.

They had a weird chemistry, he would talk about how she had a problem staying on beat while she was singing so she was recording more takes than normal and wanted to take a break.

I had respect for her and Angela Winbush both. Angela was married to Ron Isley when she came to Virginia to work. Teddy delayed started her project so many time Ron Isley called the studio as "Mr. Biggs" and told Teddy off. "Future Recording Studios Tony speaking may I help you" I answered the phone at my desk. "Yeah where's Ted" the voice on the other line demanded."Who's calling" I replied. "Tell him its Mr. Biggs" he says "Who" I ask "Mr Biggs Ron Isley put Teddy on the phone".

I don't know what Ron told him but after that call Teddy immediately went to work on Angela's project. Was this nigga Ron Isley really Mr Biggs?

Chapter 14

Meeting Michael Jackson (Again)

Teddy had been working with Michael Jackson for about a year before I started working there. From what I observed, they had mutual respect for each other and a sort of brotherly bond. Donna Moore called a meeting with everyone about a day of two before Michael was due to arrive in Virginia.

During the meeting Donna read a long ass list of what to do and what not to do in his presence. Things like no photos , don't speak to him unless he speaks to you, don't ask for autographs dont look him in the face etc etc. I was like damn, I don't even think I want to be around while he is here if it's like all of that. I had met him once in Italy in May of 1988 when I worked for CBS, Even though that first time meeting him was only a 5 minute encounter I don't remember getting all of these rules read to us back then.

Maybe Michael's people thought we would be wildin out, or maybe Donna made those rules up to keep us in check. I was there sitting in the hallway when his entourage entered the studio. It was almost mystical when he and his people entered the studio…I thought to myself…"that's got damn Michael Jackson the King of Pop, The Thriller himself" and he was cool about everything.

After my fan moment I snapped out of being enchanted by this mega star and came back to reality. "Don't look at him" I kept telling myself "be cool Tony be cool"

I had a couple of young guys from Portsmouth at the studio, Otis, Peahead and Troy and I had to make them stay in the recreation room until Michael got settled in the A-room with Teddy. I walked in the room and made the announcement…"Yo yall gotta stay in here for a few minutes and when I come back to get you we gonna leave…" "Why whats going on?" my lil homie Otis Reese asked …"Nothing is wrong I replied…Michael Jackson just came in and we need to get him settled in and then clear out the studio" I explained. "WHAT" Otis got excited "You mean to tell me that Michael Jackson is in the next room and we gotta stay in here? That's some bullshit Tony Brown!" Otis said obviously disappointed.

Michael Jackson in Virginia was a phenomena that Hampton Roads was not really ready for. We had an upcoming artist/ producer who went by the name "Screwface" who allegedly sold a tip to the media and let the press know that Michael was in Virginia recording at Future and what hotel he was staying in.

I pulled up to the studio one day and the parking lot was surrounded by news vans from every major network, they staked out the hotel where Michael was staying and the recording studio trying to catch a glimpse and interview with Michael.

Teddy was upset because we were all tight and none of the insiders would have tipped off the media..."they said they got a tip from somebody named Albert Charles" Teddy explained to me..."who the hell is Albert Charles?" I looked through the payroll files and found out that Albert Charles was "Screwface's" government name.

Michael wasn't too phased by the tip off. He went out and brought a new condo in a neighborhood in Virginia Beach that wasn't even complete. I think the unit he brought was the model. I thought to myself "Damn he brought a condo just like it was a pair of sneakers."

Our first interaction at Future was in the game room. Everybody was an avid gamer, Teddy had arcade games and television game systems and Michael was a beast at games. I guess a guy who has a whole amusement park should be okay at arcade games. Michael had been killing everybody at Joe Montana football...I was armchair coaching from the sidelines rooting for the boss of course telling Teddy to "play defense."

After Michael beat Teddy someone yelled out "Play Tony" I was pretty good at the game and would beast on people at the studio. I thought that Teddy, Markell and them must be letting him win. I ain't going to take it easy on him. I don't care if it is Michael Jackson.

I sat down to play and as I looked over at him he smiled and nuzzled down to play and Michael Jackson straight embarrassed me and teased me in the process…"is Michael Jackson talking shit to me?" I thought to myself. He must have learned a trick play or glitch in the game console and could throw a 70 or 80 yard touchdown pass in one play and he shut down every play I tried to run. "Play defense Tony" Mike started telling me what I had been telling Teddy "play defense" but he was giggling as he scored touchdown after touchdown.

We had a house rule that if you were losing by 21 to 0 you had to give up the game. He beat me 3 times 21 to nothing before quitting and going into the A-Room to work.

Markell, Tim and everyone started laughing which got me a little tight..."I bet you can't beat me". I challenged everyone else in the room but nobody wanted to play the game anymore...Thanks Michael.

Michael had a great sense of humor and when I saw him eat KFC I thought to myself..."Mikes just a normal guy" but then there was an occasion where I was like this guy aint normal. Like the time I was in the studio late one night as usual and had started to clean up because I thought everybody was gone. I walked into the recreation room which I sometimes call the pool room because the pool table was the centerpiece of the room. There was a projector screen on the far right wall and the wall on the far left of the room was covered in wall to wall mirrors.

Michael was in the pool room alone looking at himself as he danced in the huge wall to wall mirror that was on the left wall of the room. He was moving quickly with his shoulders and head as if he was trying to fake himself out in the mirror... yall know that famous "MJ" movement. "Excuse me, I didn't know you were in here" I said as I entered the room. When Michael saw me through the mirror entering the room to vacuum he spun around quickly and asked me "Tony, have you ever seen yourself in the mirror and wonder if it's really you on the other side?" then he spun back around and continued to dance in the mirror. I said "Umm no I ain't never did that one before" as I backed out of the room.

I never wanted to interrupt him or ask him for pictures or autographs, because I wanted not only him, but everyone who came to town to record to feel at ease and unbothered. I did get an autographed 8x10 before he left which has since been destroyed in a hurricane, but the memory remains.

I finished cleaning up that night and went into my office. I think Teddy was asleep and the engineers had taken a break while Teddy was asleep. When Michael was in town that would be the only time they could get some rest. Serban would sometimes sleep in the A-Room under the console and Teddy had a bedroom in the back of the A-Room.

Michael stood in the doorway of my office and said "I want to go to Walmart" I looked up in absolute shock and awe...Okay let me call Sifu and your security so we can...."We don't need security I'll wear a disguise he said? "Well let me wake Teddy to tell him we are going" ..."No don't wake him he needs his rest" Michael said. I tried to stall and buy some time to get someone to go with me, but nobody was around.

Damn! After the incident at the movies with New Kids on the Block I wanted to make sure shit went smooth but Michael insisted that we go...He put on a baseball cap and pulled the collar up on his jacket. "That's your disguise?" I asked. "Come on we'll be fine" he said. "Imma get fired" I thought to myself.

So at around 4:00am I hopped into my silver Mercedes Benz with the most iconic music star of all time to go to the 24 hour Walmart on Lynnhaven parkway in Virginia Beach. I didn't want to take the Future van because it stood out like a sore thumb so I took my car which wasn't that much more subdued. We walked around the store, and as I was pushing the cart for him Michael began tossing all sorts of stuff into the basket. The store was relatively empty so it wasn't too surprising that nobody approached us, in fact nobody even seemed to notice him. Michael brought a bunch of toys, games CDs and random stuff while we were at the store.

He didn't talk too much except to make small comments about an item he was getting "Oh this should be a fun game to take back" he'd say as he tossed it into the basket. The whole trip lasted about 45 minutes. As we were checking out of the store Michael started to flirt with the cashier. "Hi you're pretty" he said, changing his voice to be more soft like the media Michael. She nearly lost all of her color when she looked up to see who it was. Michael had a private voice and a public voice, he talked differently in the studio that was probably his private voice. Michael had me give her the address to the studio and invited her to come by.

The next day the young lady shows up at the studio. We were all in the A-Room when the doorbell rang and the security camera popped up showing a young lady at the door. Everyone looked up like who is that? When suddenly Michael said from the corner of the room "Oh She's here for me" everyone in the room quickly turned their heads in his direction. "He met her last night in Walmart" I said from the other side of the room, their heads suddenly turned in my direction. It was so funny like they were watching a tennis match.

Teddy and Michael had magical chemistry and a tremendous relationship which resulted in great music.

Chapter 15

Go Shortie Its Your Birthday

Teddy's birthday is October 8 and every year in October he did something big. From mansion parties in Miami on exclusive islands to birthday parties on million dollar yachts nothing compares or stands out to me like 1995.

In 1995 we went over the top extraordinary. We coordinated a concert with BET that took place in our own backyard and featured not only Teddy and Blackstreet but Biggie Smalls, Junior Mafia, The Luniz, Naughty By Nature, Faith Evans, Mary J Blige Wreckx N Effect and Adnia Howard.

Everybody came into town a day or so earlier and they all stopped by Future Recording studios to check in with Teddy. It was insane!

 The day leading up to that concert was crazy. Puffy and some of his Bad Boy crew had come to the studio, Biggie, Lil Cease and Faith.

Some argument sparked off between Biggie and Faith and she asked me if I could give her a ride somewhere. I didn't think anything about it and drove off with her...she wanted to take a break and just grab something simple from the store.

We were in Lynnhaven Mall on our way to a hair supply store when Faith decided to grab my arm and walk arm in arm with me though the mall. Less than 5 seconds afterwards my girlfriend Patrice walks pass..."Nigaa I thought you were supposed to be at work in Hampton and here you are in the mall with some bitch" Patrice said angrily. "Baby this aint no bitch this is Faith Evans" I started to explain "I dont give a fuck who it is nigga you got me fucked up" she said as she stormed off.

"I'm sorry" Faith offered "Big's tripping your girl's tripping they'll both be alright" Faith said re-grabbing my arm and continuing to the hair supply store to get her hair glue.

I dropped Faith off at the hotel and Craig Mack comes outside "Yo are you the runner?" he asked me "Naw dude I'm Teddy's Studio Manager" I replied "Oh shit I heard you were the weed plug" Craig answered back "I'm trying to blaze one before I get to the venue" I didn't have any weed on me at the time and told him that I'd look out for him later. I had about 10 comp tickets but 20 people who wanted to come to the show. I spent the majority of the day riding around running last minute errands and making sure my staff was good.

I made sure all staff got at least a couple of comp tickets and an extra backstage pass. I gave my 10 comp tickets away to people who I knew would not be particularly welcomed backstage and then made fake backstage passes for everyone I wanted close to me, so all of my homeboys were backstage wearing show credentials.

I would go to the 24 hour Kinkos and make color copies and laminate them for free.

One year on his birthday Teddy decided he wanted to give the entire staff white gold "Blackstreet" medallions like the one on the cover of the 2nd album. I started out ordering the necklaces and gave an invoice to Nicole to show Teddy.

Nicole came back with a list of names and varying sizes for each necklace. After seeing the invoice Teddy decided to make some of the medallions smaller in diameter and some would be cast in silver instead of white gold.

The list was interesting to say the least. Every member of the group got a larger white gold chain, along with people like Donna, Markell and Nicole, some employees like Christo, Tim and myself got a smaller white gold chain and some employees and other producers got their chains in silver. This cause a lil stir up because certain people's names were either missing from the list or they didn't get the size and quality chain they thought they deserved. They would come to me and make little comments about it, but I was like "damn...the man was giving away gifts on his birthday shut the fuck up and be thankful...What did you get him? What do you get the man who has everything for his birthday? Give him inspiration.

Miami Birthday Week Teddy went all out one year for his Birthday and the whole company made its way down to Miami for the week. Teddy rented a gigantic mansion on Star Island in Miami across the street from Gloria Estfean's house and the house that they used as Tony Montana's mansion in the movie Scarface. The place was ridiculously huge with a 4 bedroom guest house that was larger than my single family home back in Virginia. I secured a room in the main mansion and in the guest house.

The place had multiple swimming pools and a yacht parked outback. Tim and I drove down to Miami instead of flying because I wanted to take guns down. So we gassed up the Future van and hit the road trying to beat Teddy's flight. We made it and met Teddy and the rest of the guys at the airport. That week in Miami was incredible Teddy had every entertainer in the industry at his party. Uncle Luke showed us a side of Miami I will never forget. He was our liaison on day one and we ended up partying in his strip club.

We had a security guy named Shawn Bonner who was the very definition of cock diesel. He could curl these ridiculously huge dumbbells with one arm and eat 6 Chic Fil A sandwiches in one setting. Shawn was a Muay Thai fighter, I dont believe Shawn was as good of a martial artist as Sifu or myself, but he was great gentlemen and very very good at what he did. The only time I ever saw Shawn Bonner let his guard down was when we were in Miami for Teddy's birthday week. The only other time I had been to Miami was when I was in the Army and that was only for one day but this trip was a trip.

We were picking up random girls from South beach and bringing them back to Star Island and it was just because of that logo of ½ of Teddy's face being on the side of the van. "OOOOHhhh Yall work for Teddy Riley? Where He at?" "Can we go?" simple as that…most of the time Teddy would never even see these chicks or see them and nobody would claim them. The night of Teddy's birthday October 8th, we were all on this huge yacht that had about 4 levels to it.

The inner most level is where the dance floor was located. I was bouncing around between the dance floor level and the upper deck where the smoking section was... the only thing is I was smoking weed not Newports. Pookie, Keivan and I were up top smoking when Aaron Hall walked up to join the cypher.

Aaron is my man and I love that dude but I couldn't help but laugh at him whenever Teddy came topside he would throw the joint overboard. "Hey" Pookie said you threw the blunt in the water?" "Yeah man I didn't want Teddy to see me smoking" Aaaron said. Teddy hung around for a few minutes before going off to talk to someone else. Pookie rolled another blunt and we resumed our cypher when Teddy comes back uptop...this time Keivan tosses the blunt overboard. What the fuck nigaa? Pookie said pissed off that the second blunt he rolled ended up in the ocean. "I thought we was ducking Teddy with the weed" Keivan said. A lot of shit went down once that boat docked back at Star Island.

Chapter 16

Illusions and Delusions

It wasn't long before Donna, the live-in girlfriend and mother of his daughters found out about the secret honeycomb hideout that Michael had given Teddy. Teddy had another girl named Nicole move in. This was not the same Nicole his brother Markell was dating. This Nicole was a light complexion bombshell who had a little girl of her own but Teddy wasn't the father at least not to my knowledge. When Donna discovered this she went there to confront Teddy. "Tony Donna is outside of the condo bugging out" Teddy whispered over the phone.."Where are you?"

Teddy was inside of the condo watching his baby momma go nuts on the security camera. Teddy had purchased a white BMW for Nicole and Donna allegedly destroyed the vehicle in a jealous rage. A few guys went to diffuse the situation and we created a cover for Teddy saying he was in the studio the whole time. Deceitful shit.

At times there was a great deal of deceit taking place a lot of jealousy and envy in the atmosphere. It was too many women competing for Teddy's attention and they would do anything to be the standout. Every woman who came through Future Recording Studios knew who Donna Roberts was but none of them gave a fuck. They all wanted to take her place and be the one in the big house with the big ring.

But even that was an illusion when I overheard Nicole and Kareen talking one day about how the Asian nail tech pointed out that Donna's diamond wasn't real. What the fuck? This dude blows money on stupid shit all the time but his baby momma wearing fake diamonds. It was all for appearance.

A lot of things that take place with celebrities are all for appearance. One day I had been rolling around the city with Jay Z, this was way before he became the mogul he is today but Jay Z had come to Virginia to do some things with Teddy and Blackstreet while he was dribbling in VA. Jay Z was an interesting person insomuch as he was interested in what people did at the studio.

"What's his job?" Jay would ask as people were being introduced to him.

Jay Z's debut album was about to be released and his star was being polished to shine bright. I think he noticed the number of slackers just hanging around Future and wondered "why is that person even here" Seems like everybody was a runner or producer, people love to front even though my title was "manager" I would just call myself a worker.

I could do whatever needed to be done from setting up a session,to processing paperwork, to security, to event planning, to driver and even errand runner at times… you name it. I could do all things through him that strengthens me.

I earned my keep. But Jay peeped game quickly, there were a lot of people just hanging around frontin.

Like all of the artists who came to Virginia to record at Future Recording Studio Jay Z got the basic Hampton Roads tour, I showed him around the mall a few hood spots, the oceanfront etc but most of the time Jay would be with Tone Capone in the purple MVP.

I was chilling with them one day hanging out by Norfolk State University. NSU was a go to spot to pick up college girls. Suddenly my pager started going off "911 ....My girlfriend Patrice from the swimsuit model competition was now pregnant and going into labor. Tone hauled ass to get me to the hospital, and we all went in anxiously both Tone Capone and Jay Z walked in with me talking about they wanted to be the Godfather but it was a false alarm. Patrice had 3 false alarms before finally giving birth to my son Cameron Hunter Brown on October 16, 1996.

When we got back to the studio we pulled into the parking lot to see Chauncey Black outside doing something odd to his truck. Chauncey had brought a Toyota Land-cruiser but was pulling all of the Toyota logos and emblems off the car and replacing them with Lexus logos and emblems. Jay Z noticed what he was doing and fried his ass. To "fry" someone is to joke on them until they can't take it anymore...they're done. "Yo Black are you turning a Toyota into a Lexus?" We all laughed as Chauncey tried to justify the switch. A music star is supposed to be riding around in the best of the best ...it's about appearance. Jay Z and Tone Capone continued to let Chauncey have it but it was all light hearted nothing mean spirited.

C Black has a Bentley now and aint nothing fake about that. Teddy's brother Markell had decided to jump the broom and get married and yours truly was placed in charge of the Bachelor Party. I hired the baddest strippers from every strip club in the area and booked the Presidential Suite at the Marriott for Miggdie's bachelor party. Apparently Markell was more concerned about losing Nicole as his woman than losing fans, whereas Teddy stayed away from marriage. I don't think it was so much as to not disappoint female fans but I think it was his way out so he could enjoy his freedom and promiscuity.

The party needless to say was THE SHIT! Every stripper was paid in advance with an anything goes understanding. The girls were excited because all of the guys there were in the entertainment business or some sort of sports figure. We had professional boxers, R&B singers, Rap Artists, NBA players and all of Markell's homeboys from Harlem Posse Deep at the bachelor party. I had a hustler's mentality and even though I paid each stripper with an anything goes understanding I was taxing guys extra for one on one time with the girl of their choice.

"Damn bro that light skinned girl in the white who is that?" asked one prominent figure at the party…"Oh thats Creme" I replied "Is She fucking" the celeb replied "Man yeah for $500" I told him. Anxious to get that ass he gave me $500 for some one on one time with Creme. I approached Creme and told her "Yo Creme here is an extra $100 "so and so" wants some one on one time with you" passing her a $100 bill. "For real" Creams got excited "He wants ME?" "yeah" I said "go ahead and do your thing." Creme would have fucked anyone in that room for free she was a super groupie, but I looked out for her while making a lil extra for myself. Creme ended up doing 3 VIP dances that night and aside from the initial $1000 she got paid she made an extra $300 and I came out with an extra $1200 off her alone.

Jay Z peeped what I was doing and was cracking up…"you getting $500 per girl and only giving them $100…pretty slick". Jay Z stayed in Virginia through Markell Riley's wedding after which I never saw him again except in the media.

To be honest I am not in the least bit amazed at his musical accomplishments, Jigga was dope, but his business accomplishments are equally as astounding. His drive and ambition was apparent from the first time I met him.

Despite all the magic of music and seemingly glitz and glam associated with the business, the streets were vital to my survival. I had a job in the studio, but after my divorce from my first wife Zina I was getting hit for $380 a week in Child Support and my check was short. Plus Teddy cut back on everybody's income so I had taken another pay cut along with the entire staff it was hard making ends meet at times and the schedule was so varying and demanding that it was impossible to work a second job.

I had roots in the streets and dabbled in some less than legal behaviour to supplement my income at Future. Everyone had gone through several rounds of pay cuts between Blackstreet albums. I did a lot of firing, laying off and breaking bad news to people that they were being laid off. I got so upset one time I thought about quitting myself.

Teddy had me fire about 5 people a few days before Thanksgiving one year and I tried my damndest to soften the blow and offer some form of hope that when things picked financially or when royalty checks started to come in that they would be able to come back to work.

My speech worked and although they were upset there was also an air of optimism but, as I dismissed the meeting we walked outside of the studio to see a flatbed truck dropping off a brand new $100,000 car to Teddy and another delivery truck dropping off $20,000 in rims. "Oh this nigga gone fire us and buy a new car the same day" Fuck Teddy Riley one of them would say as they left the lot. I stood there watching them unload the vehicle and watching Teddy come outside all smiling and happy while good people like Ms Delaney and Spooge who had just been fired walked to the bus stop.

I felt so bad knowing that those people could have stayed on payroll until after the Thanksgiving and Christmas holidays if Teddy had waited on buying another luxury sports car. This nigga was selfish and I was starting to see it more and more. He didn't want nobody to have a better car, a prettier woman, a longer chain, nothing. Damn. It was for reasons such as this that I always felt the need to "supplement" my income and get my own money.

Aside from brokering transactions for various substances, I picked up a Robin Hood mentality and started jacking certain so called "hustlers".

Once after Rodeo and some of his friends from the Beach came through and won a few thousand dollars gambling against Teddy and Markell...cheating. Without anyone noticing, I left the studio while the game was still in progress and squatted on them waiting for them to leave. I caught them slipping about a mile away from the studio and took all of their shit... jewelry, money and car keys too. This wasn't something that I did often. I just did it a few times to a few guys who showed off too much or guys who came to the studio and saw us as victims and thought that they could take advantage of Teddy and Markell. Plus the dude had smashed my girl and I didn't like him anyway.

There were a lot of hustlers around the studio and everybody was flossy because they all wanted to give the appearance that they had money like Teddy. The Life Of Riley. My street crew was through and not to be fucked with. Vito Mitchell, Troy Mitchell, Tabari Anthony, John Mitchell were my aces. My main man from Portsmouth was Fred Mitchell aka Hootie Bang. Bang and I grew up in the same housing projects in Portsmouth Va called Jeffery Wilson Housing Projects which we called J-Dub or just "The Dub."

We were both high school wrestlers and football players, but he was 2 years ahead of me.

Bang went to Wilson High School and I went to Manor High school, the same school Missy Elliot attended, but I had graduated a few years before her. Bang was an ex-Navy guy who had been jumped into the Crips when he was stationed in Long Beach, California.

A jump in is when the member of a gang fights you as a form of initiation. Bang did some work with Snoop Dogg, Warren G and The Twins back in Cali and was rolling with the Crips. All my people were Bloods but I operated independently. Bang and I were brothers from P-Town and that bond surpassed everything. Shit had gotten so bad around Future financially for me at one point that one day Bang and I decided to pull a sting.

We planned the whole thing but when it was time to do the job we unexpectedly saw an off duty police officer in the area and that caused us to divert our actions. We hit a lick elsewhere and got away with two bags full of money. Well one bag was full of money the other was full of Food Stamp coupons.

I had another homeboy named Big Leon. Big Leon was a New York / Virginia hybrid who dabbled in the street enough to finally go legit. He had a little corner grocery store in downtown Norfolk smack dab in the hood and Hootie Bang and I got him to buy the Food Stamps, but the best deal he could give us was 35 cents on the dollar for the exchange.

I felt so fucked up after jacking hustlers and hitting licks, it was easy, but doing that it was too much of a risk and I wasn't trying to go back to jail. Bang didn't slow down and eventually he'd get caught and sentenced to 5 years in Federal Penitentiary. One might wonder, "why in the hell would you pull stings and jack drug dealers while you were working for one of the top music producers in the world", simple, he wasn't paying us enough.

Money was coming in I know for sure, I would get the royalty statements from songs that Teddy had made years earlier and the checks were fat, plus he was charging up to $100,000 a track production fees. Money was definitely coming in but it wasn't going out properly anymore... Tim and I had started splitting money from the vending machines in the hallway and replacing brand named snacks with generic chips and sodas.

Everybody had complaints about what they were being paid thinking that Teddy was not being fair, but I never complained about pay and I understood the number of people he was responsible for and the pressure he was under. But I still can't help but think that had he cut fat from other areas, like taking care of so many stray chicks, he would have been fine. Teddy maintained employees who earned their money, family members who expected money and women who wanted money.

His wallet was getting tighter but I had to get mine regardless. Gene Griffin came to Virginia with Aaron and Damion Hall when they were supposed to be putting GUY back together. Gene Griffin was notorious. He came in and invited me to lunch one day. During that lunch meeting Gene gave me a lot of game. He basically told me how he and Teddy first met and much more than I needed to or cared to know.

I had gained more respect for him after the meeting. People had made him out to be a bad guy but he was on the level with me. Gene told me that the touring equipment was insured by the label and came out of a tour support budget so if anything was ever broken or missing just file a claim and get a new piece of equipment. I filed a claim with the label for a broken keyboard once and the company sent a new one and never asked for the broken item to be returned.

This gave me the idea to sell off the old tour equipment and replace it with new gear through the label's insurance company. Between tours I took all of the old keyboards that the band had been using out of the Jack Rabbit Storage unit we had and sold them to Sam Ash Music store in New York, I would then file a claim with the girl at the label and go to Audio Light and Musical in Norfolk, Virginia to get new equipment in time for the next tour.

Years later someone told Teddy I was stealing gear, but I controlled the inventory and nothing ever came up missing. A few studio employees benefited from the sale of old equipment ...Tim Smith used to call it bonus time. I would look out for all of the lowest paid studio workers and include them from time to time, Keivan, Pookie, Lil Chris we all ate off the resale of old used equipment when payroll was funny.

For a while Keivan Pookie and I could be considered the 3 amigos. We rolled together all the time because we were smokers and didn't give a fuck what Teddy thought about weed smokers. Keivan was Eric Williams' cousin and Pookie was Teddy's cousin. I was told by Teddy to fire them both on numerous occasions but would always find a way to make him change his mind.

I think Keivan annoyed Teddy because he was always trying to find a reason to fire him. Keivan felt it too and soon he was like as long as my cousin Eric is around I'm good.

"Tony Keivan messing with one of the dancers …fire him. Hey Tony Keivan stole my gun …fire him, Hey Tony Keivan took a deep breath today …fire him". It was ridiculous. Pookie was Teddy's blood relative and he expected me to fire him too.

"Teddy I'm not comfortable firing your family members man …all they do is come back to you and say Tony fired me and you give them their jobs right back". Pookie lived in the Boggs house with Will Skylz, Kaseem Coleman and Lil Chris Smith. I had the spare room on the 3rd floor. We used to call the Boggs house "The PLAYER'S PALACE" because of the number of girls that we shuffled through there.

For whatever reason, we always had strippers around and girls with little inhibitions. It would be nothing to knock on the door and have a naked woman greet you upon entry.

One day Kaseem left the house and did not pull the door closed tightly, this set off the alarm causing the police to respond. Once the police arrived they sent a K-9 into the house to secure the property. The dog alerted on Pookie's room after detecting the odor of weed and locked the Boogs house down. Keivan was upstairs in my room when the cops came and called me. "Yo I have a box of hand grenades upstairs in that room, take them out and leave through the back exit" I explained to him.

Keivan took the grenades out of the house and put them in the middle of the back yard and placed a plastic trash can over them. That stood out like a sore thumb. Luckily the cops didn't find any weed in Pookies room nor did they find my box of grenades.

A high point of me working at Future cam when I got a chance to meet my grandmother's favorite white man next to JFK...I'm talking about none other that Tom Jones.

As a kid, I used to watch The Tom Jones Show with my grandmother sitting on the hardwood floors on an mat watching this white girls go crazy over this guy. When Tom Jones walked in I looked around for him thinking that he would enter following the other two little ole white guys. Tom introduced himself, "I'm Tom Jones" he said, extending his hand for a greeting.

After a closer look I said to myself "damn that lil ole dude really is Tom Jones." He looked nothing like his celebrity self. He had a gut, thin hair and was pale and wrinkly. He was in town to do a cover of Prince's song "Kiss" but he had also had a concert booked for Chrysler Hall while he was in town. I set up the studio for them to begin recording but didn't stay for the whole session.

I left to run some errands and when I returned Tom had finished his vocal and was in the guest bathroom changing for his show. When he walked out of the restroom he was the Tom Jones I remember.

Tom had went in and put on his girdle, spray tan toupee and sequins and was ready to rock. I asked him over the period of his career how many pairs of panties did he think he collected from female fans throwing their underwear at him...Tom replied laughingly "enough to start my own lingerie department at the biggest department store you guy have around here" I believed him too Tom Jones was at one time THE MAN.

Chapter 17

1996 Another Level

By the time touring to support and promote the first album had finished, the group would undergo reconstruction once again. Mark Middleton came in to replace Levi and Eric Williams came in to replace Dave Hollister.

My first impression of Mark Middleton left the lasting impression that he is a great guy; he was a very GOD fearing guy who was soft spoken and had a love for boxing. Mark could talk boxing with you for hours and knew a bunch of minute details about fighters that nobody else knew.

Mark was very physically fit, had those R&B singer looks and great disposition. We had a tattoo party one night at the studio and Mark decided to get a tattoo of a lion on his chest, but the pain was so excruciating that he quit mid way through.

I wonder if he ever got that finished. That same night I got a tattoo of a dragon and Teddy got a tat of a huge cross on his back with the words "Forgiven" tatted above the cross. "Who the hell forgave him" Sifu whispered to me jokingly as he walked by.

Eric Williams also known as E-Ballad or as I call him E-Class, was a dope singer who was involved in the early Hip Hop R&B stuff like singing the hook on LL COOL J's "Around The Way Girl'.

Eric and I quickly became friends, he has a warm personality, very humble and down to Earth. When Eric came to Virginia he brought his cousin Keivan Willaims too and Keivan and I bonded like brothers instantly. That's my man til this day. Keivan was the classic NYC street guy. Anyone who has ever met a New Yorker knows they have a certain swagger about themselves. Kevian was no exception.

Eric also brought a production team to VA with him Wes and Kent. These guys from New Jersey who had been working on hot new music and from a small condo in Virginia Beach they began production on Jaheem's first album, I hung around Wes Kent from time to time and Jaheem a little but the few occasions that I spent around him he started shoplifting and I wasnt trying to get embarrassed and locked up fucking with this guy. He'd walk out of stores with clothes on and eat food while walking around the grocery stores, not giving a fuck. Nonetheless Eric, Wes and Kent did a great job on Jaheem's debut album.

The success Jaheim enjoyed as a solo artist could have easily been Eric William's success but E was dedicated to the group, even at time when they couldn't tour because Teddy had to stay back and produce for someone else, Eric ate it with a side of dissent. How was Teddy producing for GUY and all of these other acts benefiting Eric's situation? It wasn't.

His cousin Keivan was a typical NYC hustler. He had some shit with him but we were on the same shit so it was all good. Keivan pulled one of the coveted Blackstreet dancers and made her his girl and she was loyal which pissed a couple group members off. There were at least 3 occasions where Teddy talked to me about firing Keivan but I always had Keiv's back because the reasons were always bullshit.

Always some nonsense about a stolen pistol or girl. According to Teddy Keivan stole his pistol at least 4 times and each time he insisted that I fire him but the gun was eventually found somewhere around the studio, in a car or at Teddy's house. And of course after it was made clear that Kareema was not messing with nobody but Keivan that would really piss him off. Someone he thought of as a "regular guy" got one of the girls he wanted or had his eye on. He would eliminate any competition. But in all fairness, a lot of women just objectified him too…he and a few of the other guys were just some woman's chance to sleep with a celebrity, meanwhile dudes like me, Pookie (Juluis McKelvey another one of Teddy's cousins) Tim Smith could pretty much pull who we wanted, but with a whole different type of swag. We were not celebrities, but I dated a couple. We were all young and handsome in our own right, and we each had an edge that them singing cats didn't have.

Once a car load of girls drove from the Eastern Shore to Virginia Beach to meet Teddy but his girlfriend Donna and the kids pulled up and Teddy couldn't get away so they ended up around my house with me Pookie and Sifu. Every time they came back it was to see me and Sifu, their celebrity crush had worn off.

Between completing the tour for the second album and recording the third album, Mark Middleton had been put out of the group too. Mark Middleton was put out simply, because he stood up for himself. He was promised things and those promises were never delivered.

Teddy made up an alternative reality about Mark messing with one of the women he was messing with but when it was all said and done Mark was done too. And that brother could sing his ass off. Throughout 1995 and 1996 production for Blackstreet's second album would be under way and a number of people would contribute to the success of this project. Writers such as Beverly Crowder, Karen Anderson Dezo were instrumental on this album.

Karen Anderson was very talented songwriter, with a lot of sex appeal. She was very curvaceous and attracted a lot of male attention from guys at the studio   Darryl Adams aka Dezo was the lead singer of the groups Basic Black and 911 and my good friend. After Basic Black another group created by Gene Griffin to replace GUY split up Dezo ended up in Virginia working with Teddy. Dezo was a good producer and singer and he was a very cool guy, but he wore his heart on his sleeve and was very emotional.

I lived with Dezo for a few months after my divorce and after a period of him joking me for moping around he got mad one day when he came home from the studio and saw me in a threesome with the 2 white girls from across the street. I had no idea that Dezo was interested in them, but was reluctant to approach them. They just came over and got naked I didn't put any romance or effort into banging them and Dezo was taking the gentlemen's approach. My Bad.

When he came into the house his eyes got as wide as dinner plates. I could see he was angry and something was wrong. "Yo Let me speak to you in the other room" Dezo explained to me how he liked one of the girls and tried to make me feel bad because she had her titles out in the living room…"Dezo I dont give a fuck about them bitches bro that was rebound sex" I went back into the living room and told them finish up with Dezo I had somewhere to go. I left the house and went out for a ride leaving the two girls and Dezo behind.

Dezo must have felt disrespected and he brought a gun into work the next day telling someone that it was for me. He should have learned his lesson after Gene Griffin pistol whipped him for something similar but apparently he wanted to test me, so I walked into the A-room where he was sitting, He had his gun sitting on the table, a pretty ass .45. I took Dezo's gun and dismantled it leaving it in pieces on the producer's console in the A-Room. "Man put my gun back together" he said angrily. "Okay let me go get mine first then I'll show you how to put yours back together".

Despite all the fussing he and I did, Dezo was another guy who grew to be like a real brother to me. My mom liked him, his mom liked me. After leaving Future amidst a slew of issues with Teddy, Dezo went on to work with Justin Timberlake before his untimely passing in 2019.

I drove from Virginia to Georgia to attend Dezo's funeral. He was laid to rest in a most beautiful place and his voice, which was equally as beautiful will live on forever.

There were some women who I felt like Teddy was just doing wrong like Lamenga Kafi, I love Lamenga. She is an amazing lady with such a beautiful voice and disposition and in my opinion was one of the sexiest women around Future

Recording studios. Lamenga was a true Southern Belle from Alabama who Teddy picked to be a part of the female equivalent to Blackstreet called "8th Ave" along with Tyvee and Beverly.

Lamenga was always around the studio writing and trying to contribute to the creative process. She had a great deal of talent and creativity yet she too would end up getting played by Teddy and eventually leaving Future Recording Studio to embark on her own endeavors.

William Stewart aka Will Skylz was one of the dopest beat makers I've ever witnessed and he did it so effortlessly. Will could do a complete beat in under 15 minutes on the MPC. Will Skillz was a big light skinned guy from New York who wore glasses and loved to eat.

By day Will would be holed up in his second floor bedroom of the Bogg's House banging away on his drum machine by night we would be out cruising the oceanfront strip hitting up after hour spots. One of those spots was the iHop down the street from the studio.

Everyone in the restaurant knew our entire staff from the numerous late night iHop runs we would often make. It was a mini spectacle when Teddy took the team out to eat at little spots like this. Always a lot of onlookers. The thing I like best about Will is he never showed his credentials. Everybody would be quick to tell a girl "I'm a producer" or "I work for Teddy Riley" but Will was low key and just as effective by distancing himself from the he-whores at Future.

Will met the woman who would eventually become his wife at that Ihop. Will worked on Blackstreet and Queenpen's album while he was living in VA. His biggest contribution was the foundation for one of Blackstreet's biggest hits "No Diggity".

Sprague Williams one of the Georgia boys was a critical component to the touring success of Blackstreet, In addition to working in the studio as a producer, Sprague also toured with Wreckx-N-Effect and Blackstreet and a keyboard technician.

I can recall one tour date Sprague was in Australia with Wreckx-N-Effect and The Pirates and a huge fight broke out and had it not been for Sprague thighs would have ended up way different. They guys in Wreckx-N-Effect had went to Australia without Sifu and after the fight broke out Teddy got the idea to send some of his "tough guy" buddies to Australia. "Imma send Scotty over there," Teddy said. "Teddy, Scotty is a shooter he can't fight" I remember Christo telling him.

Serban Ghenea, George Mayers and John Haynes were the engineers on payroll for the creation of the second album. I did a lot of engineering tasks, but never sought credit for any of it. I was more focused on project management.

Roosevelt Harrcll aka Bink Dog is another noted producer who cut his production chops at Future Recording Studios. Bink worked on songs like "Don't Leave doing some programming and contributed to some of the many remixes that were released. Pookie used to flirt with Bink's sister and that would piss Bink off, but he wouldn't do anything. Bink was more of a jokester back then, but he found a lot of success as a producer working with cats like Jay Z and many others.

The second album contains the songs:

"This Is How We Roll" which introduces Eric Williams as a vocal lead in the group and we get our first taste of Mark Middleton's mighty vocal, but the song was mundane and did not have a great impact on the album.

"No Diggity". Between the first and second albums various producers and artists came in to do remixes. Hip Hop Icon LL Cool Jay came in for about a week to work on some of the remixes. Meeting LL was epic. LL was that dude in the early days of Hip Hop. When I was recording in

Europe my label wanted me to be a hybrid of LL Cool J. I even wrote a verse back in the day to take a shot at his song "BAD" it went "Bigger and Deffer its the Brown skinned brother, B-Boy I'm hot unlike no other, BAD as can be on the M.I.C. and baby doll best believe its Tony B" ...glad it never came out ....,LL was very friendly despite his huge level of celebrity. We took the traditional trip to Military Circle Mall in Norfolk Virginia where every celebrity who came into town wanted to go LL Cool Jay arrived to sheer pandemonium with no security except me and Pookie.

He probably signed about 50 autographs in 15 minutes, After we left the mall we hung out and played a few games of pick-up basketball in the studio parking lot while we waited for Teddy to arrive.

I wondered to myself why he was so fidgety every

time a car pulled up he acted as if someone was looking for him. When it was time to hit the booth LL was the truth. He was free styling on a version of "I Like The Way You Work" and then started chanting "I like the way you work kid..No Diggity, I got to bag it up...I like the way you work kid no diggity go head and back it up". That freestyle for one song became the hook of the 2nd album's standout song "No Diggity".

Developing the video concept for No Diggity was a brainstorming session between me and Teddy. Teddy wanted to use a little puppet like the one Nike was using for the Penny Hardaway commercials. I contacted the company that made the marionettes and got a price quote. $15,000 for a puppet!

WOW! "I wanna be a puppet too" Chauncey got wind of the video concept and wanted to be featured as a marionette as well, however the budget did not allow for another $15,000 puppet. We scaled back the amount of moving parts for Chauncey's puppet to lower the price. The other 2 guys (Eric and Mark) didn't get puppets made but they didn't push the issue either.

The song became a huge hit with Dr. Dre doing the opening verse and Teddy's artist Queen Pen doing a rap break mid way through the song. No Diggity hit number 1 on Billboard Top 100 and received a Grammy for Best R&B Performance by a Rap Group or Duo and is recognized by MTV as one of the 100 Greatest Pop Songs.

Even though Teddy and I did the treatment for the video and I hand drew the storyboards, Hype Williams was hired to produce the video which was nominated for a 1998 MTV Video Music Award. It's still blows my mind to have witnessed this song grow from Will Skylz first making the beat in his bedroom where he sampled Bill Withers song Grandma's hands, to LL COOL Jay inadvertently writing the hook, to it becoming acknowledged by Q magazine as number 407 of the best 1001 songs ever made. Now while Teddy was making a decision on what to do with the beat portion of the song, Will sent a copy to Deathrow and a very similar version of the track was offered to Tupac.

Tupac recorded his song "Toss It Up" and disses Dr Dre on the track which just happened to feature Aaron Hall of Teddy's group GUY along with KiC and Jo Jo from Joedeci. Teddy sang leads on "No Diggity" but he also contributed to the song **"Fix"** which in my opinion was one of his best non vocorder vocal performances. Teddy seems to be defining a vocal style on Fix but its

Mark's intro that stabs through just in time to save the song from being regular. Elements from Grandmaster Flash "The Message" made the beat familiar enough to be a hot track and it turned out to be a banging song. Fix is probably one of my favorite Blackstreet uptempo songs probably because of the bond I developed with Ol' Dirty Bastard who came to Virginia to do the remix. O.D.B. was at the time one of the most recognizable members of Wu-Tang Clan and my man 50 grand.

Dirty whose real name was Russel Jones was a wild boy and as real as real gets. When I first met him he was sleep on the sofa in the studio lobby I walked in and tried to walk out without disturbing him…he sat up and said "yo where's the weed my nigga? "Huh" I replied a little surprised, because I was very discreet about smoking weed around the studio but this dude had micro sensors in his nostrils. "You smell like weed nigga fire it up" he said but just then Teddy came in to get him to start recording. "Yo I can't work without no weed" he exclaimed. Teddy replied "Man I don't allow anyone to smoke in here" "WHAT? FUCK THAT ...We gonna have to go to another studio" Dirty said taking off the headphones and walking out of the booth.

Teddy turned to me and said "Tony do you know how to get weed?" I laughed inside because there had not been one day when I didn't have access to weed my people and I had pounds and pounds of it. I said "I can try to get him something" Dirty dropped the headphones and said "I'm riding with him".

 I got into my Benz with Ol Dirty Bastard and drove from Virginia Beach to Portsmouth to get an ounce of weed for him. As soon as we left the studio parking lot I fired up a blunt and Russel Jones and Tony Brown became buds.

We stopped in all of the hood spots after riding around smoking and when we got back to the studio the results of the song came out great. I met up with Dirty from time to time at different events and he always showed me mad love. Once we were in Miami this time at Prince's nightclub Glam Slam. Prince wasn't there but Dirty was drunk as fuck and had gotten escort out by security.

He rarely traveled with any security or entourage even though Wu-Tang was a huge hip hop group, Ol Dirty kept it raw. I ended up walking him back to the hotel where he was staying with his arm around my neck singing Rick James songs loud and off key walking down Collins Ave.

"Good Lovin" was a dope ass song with Chauncey Black on the leads the groove of the song was just a real mellow vibe and the lyrics were meaningful and the melody was familiar because it came from a song that had already been a hit. Sherri Blair was one of the song writers on that song. Sherri was another one of the beautiful young ladies working around Future Recording Studios. Quiet and soft spoken Sherri wasn't one of the aggressive girls like the dancers or other performers. She had a talented pen game and also wrote the song ***"Let's Stay In Love"*** a beautiful ballad that Chauncey sang leads on. ***"Don't Leave"*** is another song that I watch develop from a thought into a hit. An upcoming producer at the time named Bink Harrel did some drum programming over a sample of Debarge's hit song "A Dream" and songwriter

Karen Anderson help write what is in my opinion the most beautiful song in the entire Blackstreet repertoire.

From Eric's smooth sultry intro "Nah Baby Nah Baby" to Mark's powerful ad libs, the song has a great balance of participation. Everybody got to shine, even Teddy's voice in the vocorder on the hook is critical to the success of this hit but it gave Mark and Eric a chance to make their mark in Blackstreet indefinite just as Dave had did with "Before I Let You Go" and Levi had done with "Joy" "Don't Leave" was the best song on the 2nd Album.

Mark also stood out on the song **"Never Gonna Let You Go"** which was another sultry love song written in part by Sherri Blair. Mark's voice invokes chills and goosebumps. Teddy masterfully crafted this beat and then gave it to Sherri to do her thing. I would always see her with a pen and pad in hand Sherri was not playing with her writing game.

"I Wanna Be Your Man" was written by Karen Anderson, and Teddy and Sprague Doogie worked on the production its a nice album track but the song wasn't a standout in my opinion.

"My Paradise" was a sweet song that showed a jazzy side to the group with Take 6 style harmonies and every vocalist getting an opportunity to showcase their prowess.

"Money Can't Buy Me Love" was a remake of the Beatles song and Chauncey Black sang the lead vocals, I remember walking out of the studio whenever they worked on this song for some reason I didn't like it…I think it was the tempo and pacing of the song. Turning an uptempo song from the Beatles into a Ballard didn't work out too well in my opinion. People brought into the idea of it and I think, because Michael Jackson owned the Beatles catalog Teddy probably got a sweet deal on the licensing.

I had a homeboy who was a radio personality named Morris "The Hawk" Baxter. They used to call him "The Hawk" because he would make a hawk sound on air as part of his personality. I called Morris and told him about an interview idea Teddy had and Morris was ecstatic when he found out Teddy wanted to use his voice on an interlude song called **"Blackstreet On The Radio."**

The track "Blackstreet on the Radio" was a little piece to explain the change in group members and introduce the two new members of the group. It worked well for the fans.

Another song from this album which was under-ratted was **"*I Cant Get You Out of My Mind*"** Written in part by Eric Williams and Wes Hodges this song gave Blackstreet a edgy twist. I say written in part in a lot of these cases because some writers contributed, but were not credited and some people have writers credits on these songs just for publishing credits.

"I'll Give It To You" was an album filler written by Sherri Blair this was a song I was surprise that made the album considering all the material they had to choose from. I wouldn't skip it on the playlist, but I would talk during it. "Happy Song" was a Michael Jackson feeling song that Michael had nothing to do with, The song which was written in part by Karen Anderson Teddy and Mark Middleton borrows melody ideas from Michael's Off the Wall and "I'm Every Woman" by Chaka Khan. Mark's falsetto is a nice touch to

keep the song interesting.

"The Motherlude" is simply a beautiful message from the mothers of each member of the group. I met Chauncey's mom and Teddy's mother but never any of the other group members' mothers. Teddy's mom Mother Riley as she was affectionately called around the studio was a wonderful lady who had a great welcoming spirit. She "sonned" me and every other guy around there meaning she took me in like a son.

I was stressed out about something so bad once that I had gotten a bald spot in my hair about the size of a quarter. Mother Riley noticed it and gave me a old school remedy to correct it. I have a full head of hair to this day thanks to her.

It was people like Teddy and Markell's mom Mother Riley, Nicole's mom Mother Rembert, Donna Moms. Ms Bobbie that made the organization feel more like a family atmosphere and less like a job. Honoring one's mother was a perfect way to segue into the last song on the album which was a gospel song called **"The Lord Is Real"** where everybody got a chance to go to church vocally.

Chapter 18

Teaching them Everything You Know

Now with the second Blackstreet album finished the time to hit the road doing some promo dates was at hand but there was always an abundance of paperwork that had to be completed for each song on the album, from sample clearances to licenses to writer splits it was time to get productive on the business side of the album. There were a lot of employees and interns who wanted to really learn the behind the scenes workings of the studio and music business.

Kim Smith was an intern from my alma mater Norfolk State University who was interested in learning engineering. Kim was a very voluptuous, attractive and ambitious young lady who was somewhat naive and innocent acting but she was smart and willing to absorb everything. Lucy Washington was Teddy's cousin and she was another one who was willing to absorb everything there was to know but Teddy would keep her distant for some reason.

Her brother Christo also was capable of running the facility. Christo like myself was an ex cop who was just as disciplined as I was and was learning things from me but, what I did was not glamorous, it was tedious and meticulous and soon my students of the game would fade off to the pool room to shoot pool or dice with the celebrities and their guests rather than work on paperwork in the cut.

I was more so trying to teach people who didn't want to learn so it was easier for me to just do things myself. I was taking a bunch of 2 inch reels from the studio to the climate controlled storage unit one day when Teddy saw me loading the reels into the van. "Tony I want you to start showing Madaline and Chauncey how to run the studio and do some of that paperwork so you can have some help and come on the road sometimes," Teddy told me.

Chauncey who was standing beside Teddy looked just as surprised as I did. Chauncey had absolutely no intention of managing a studio…"Nigga I'm a singer I aint no studio manager" Chauncey said to me. "I don't know why he wants me to learn this shit".

I had the underlying feeling that he wanted to phase me out more than get me help. Chauncey would eventually open his own studio but at the height of his career as an artist he wasn't trying to hear that.

Maddy was cute, but she had her own agenda and I wasn't mad at her. I was trying to maintain my connections and feed my kids. I had outside projects that I was becoming involved with.

In addition to learning how to do paperwork and run the studio a few people wanted to learn Martial Arts from either me or Sifu. Sifu was a more skilled practitioner and I often assisted him with classes he held at his home but I also trained police officers at a training academy on the boulevarde. One day I was teaching a private lesson in Escrima which is Philipino Stick Fighting to my man Screwface in the parking lot of the Recording Studio and accidentally split his eyebrow with the stick. I felt so bad because I had never hit a student hard enough to draw blood but dude was psyched up and wanted to learn more. He thought I did it on purposes for tipping the media about MJ being in town but it was a honest accident.

I didn't mind sharing my knowledge with the team, anything that I was good at that somebody wanted to learn I was willing to teach them. I didn't see anyone I taught or shared knowledge with as competition regardless of their motives.

Chapter 19

Another Level Tour

With tour time looming the band came back to Virginia to rehearse. It was good to have familiar faces around and I admired each of the musicians individual talents, especially **Loren Dawson** and Gerald Heyward. Loren is probably one of the best keyboard players I've ever met next to Bernie Worrell and Gerald was by far the best drummer I know. These guys were the heartbeat of the band

and always had great personal energy. We had a few rehearsal spots around town this time, the dancers were rehearsing in a dance studio on Bonney Road and the group used the both the live room to sequence the show order and then dress rehearsals were at the theater over at Hampton University.

I went out with the group to a New Years Eve performance on December 31 1996 where they opened up followed by New Edition and then Keith Sweat. Blackstreet absolutely shut the show down because of the production effort that went into the performance. Teddy knew how to put on a show and as an opening act they fucked New Edition and Keith Sweat up that night, It was like being at a true live concert when Blackstreet was on stage, and then going to a night club to listen to New Edition and Keith Sweat. N.E. and Keith were on point that night but the band that Teddy put together gave Blackstreet an edge on their performance.

I remember standing on the side with Mike Bivins of New Edition watching Blackstreet perform. "Teddy showing out tonight" Mike said "they came like they were the headliners." A few weeks later at the Superdome in Tampa Florida New Edition opened for Blackstreet.

New Edition came with a music director and a track performance and of course Blackstreet travelled with a full band, a drummer, 2 keyboard players, bass player, guitar player and 4 dancers. In addition to the performers other individuals were crucial to these live performances Sprague was the sound tech , Butch, Tim Miller and Bongo were the roadies, Sifu headed security and sometime took a second with him. So there were a number of people on the road when the group left.

This created a hefty touring expense that at times may have exceeded the touring budget. Teddy thought to optimize his availability and had the brilliant idea to put a recording studio on a tour bus. This would resolve the issue of him not being able to tour with Blackstreet because of his production schedule. The studio bus was awesome... it had all of the equipment he needed to produce plus better sleeping space than his closet in the A-Room.

The bus stayed parked in front of the studio until it was time to hit the road. Teddy started to spend more and more time on the bus to hide away and duck people looking for him in the studio. The extra production space gave him the solitude he needed to be creative. The bus was a great idea for the U.S. date but Teddy soon discovered that the vehicle was too large for the roads in Europe AFTER he shipped it over. Who's dumb ass idea was that? Nobody thought to check?

By the summer of 1997 Blackstreet was one of the hottest acts out and one of the biggest events in music was about to go down. Summer Jam. Teddy took the bus to New York in June of 97 for the Hot 97 Summer Jam show. I followed them in the Future van with a few of my friends from the hood. Everybody wanted to go to Summer Jam because everybody who had a song on the radio was there performing. The money wasted shipping the studio bus to Europe was a huge waste.

By the end of this tour Blackstreet would say bye bye to Mark Middleton and hello to Terrell Phillips. "What happened with Mark? I asked "Oh he tried to fuck one of Teddy's girls on tour or something" Tim replied "What" this shit is getting ridiculous." Truth of the matter was that Mark demanded his money and Teddy found a petty reason to let him go. Someone asked you think it was a money over bitches thing? No, I think Mark wanted his money in the midst of some dispute about a girl.

Teddy was good at diverting a conversation away from money to other shit. We had another famous budget cut meeting and during this meeting Earl got fed up with taking the pay cuts and blurted out "But What About Me Royalties?" "What royalties? " Teddy responded…Earl explained "My song made it onto the "Blank Man" movie…I ain't see no money yet" And Earl was right, these checks had been came in, but weren't being disbursed properly. Teddy gave Nicole's responsibility to Maddy and Lucy's responsibilities and pretty much mine too… So things were being done …well, let's just say differently.

I remember in a meeting Teddy promised to give Eric and Mark $500,000 each after Interscope released the budget for the third album which would be the "Finally" album ,but after the money came in he only gave them $100,000 each instead. What about Chauncey? By that time it was speculated that C Black had money from another source, one which I won't touch on out of respect to his family. Before this, the group came back from a trip to LA to meet with Jimmy Iovine at Interscope and I noticed both Teddy and Chauncey were sporting black pinky nails on one hand.

What kinda shit is that I asked Eric where's your black pinky nail? I aint doing that shit Eric replied. What does that mean? Ask them niggas he said. I asked Chauncey he just laughed and made up all kinda stupid shit. Neither of them would tell me what the black pinky nail represented and I wondered if NOT getting that Black pinky cost Eric and Mark not to get the full amount they were promised.

Chapter 20

1998 The beginning of the end

The beginning of the end for me came in 1998 when Teddy started giving jobs to Chauncey's relatives and started to have this hispanic soothsayer voodoo bitch come through the studio talking about she was doing a "cleansing." This lady was trying to draw a circle around Sprague one day thinking he was asleep when Sprague opened his eyes and told her to get the hell away from him.

Things just started to get weirder and weirder. Teddy hired Chauncey Black's little brother who I absolutely rocked with and his brother-in-law who turned out to be an asshole.

The problem was that Chauncey's people came thinking that they didn't have to do the tasks assigned to them. His little brother was cool and did what he was supposed to do but his brother-in-law Jeff was feeling himself a little too much and it was on the day of October 20th 1998 that he decided to diss me in my office and try to buck on my authority when I slammed him through my glass desk causing such a huge commotion that Sifu and Christo ran back to my office to break it up.

Mary J Bilge was in town to record. I walked in the A Room and introduced myself to her and get sister. Mary said I had a great "aura" and asked if I could take them to a few places.

At the time, I had no idea what she was talking about but this was a chance to hang with Mary J Bilge, I wasn't turning it down... besides Teddy wasn't ready to record just then so we had a few hours to spare. I spent the majority of the day escorting Mary J and her sister around to different places. A few hours later Teddy called me and asked to get a 2inch reel to reel tape from storage.

I called Earl who was on duty as a runner and asked him to go and get the tape before Teddy got there. "Okay Mon I got it" Earl replied to me. A few more hours go by and after hitting up a few shopping malls with Mary, I headed back to the studio. Teddy and Earl were standing in the hallway with Big Wayne, Sifu, Christo and a few other guys. "Earl did you give Teddy the reel I asked..."Naw Mon, the kid Jeff done gone with the van" Earl said..I could see Teddy was irritated. "Use my car and go get it Earl" I gave Earl the key to my car to run down the street to the storage unit and get the tape.

I went back to my office to call Jeff but didn't get an answer. Mary got ready to leave and as I took her back to the hotel she started telling me she could see a person's aura and that my aura was welcoming but Teddy's seemed a little off.

I dropped her back off at the hotel and returned to the studio. Jeff was back by then and I asked could I see him in my office. He told me he used the studio van to ride round and holler at bitches. Something Teddy got rid of his own brother in law for doing. I tried to school Jeff but the conversation got heated when he told me he works for Teddy and Chauncry and not me. "So fuck what I say huh?" I said as I stood up from my desk."Not only that fuck you too" Jeff replied....It was at that point that things got physical and Jeff ended up getting slammed across the glass desk.

"What the fuck is going on back here?" Christo yelled as he ran into the room. Sifu grabbed me and Christo stood between me and Jeff. The 12 gauge pump that was mounted to the bottom of my desk was on the floor and I picked it up and placed it on the file cabinet. Jeff got up and went into the hallway where Teddy was..."That Nigga crazy" Jeff kept saying. "That nigga crazy."

Teddy was annoyed at everything by then and told both Jeff and I to leave and it was at that very moment that I decided to quit. I had had enough "Leave?!? man fuck you Teddy I quit how the fuck you gonna ask me to leave?" I said angrily.

"Quit then people tired of you bullying them around anyway" Teddy replied.."I pay you more than anyone around here when I tell you to do something do it" Teddy bossed up on me. "Yo Teddy before I snap the fuck out let me get my shit and bounce" I said as I walked back to my office to get my belongings particularly my weapons.

As I walk toward my office I hear "Don't make me earn my check today" said Big Wayne..."Big Wayne I will fuck you up" I said as I started towards him. Big Wayne was a former professional wrestler in the WWF but he had bad knees and could barely stand up. His statue was very intimidating but he was washed up. One inside kick to his patella and he would be done. Sifu stepped in and intervened "Wayne Tony Brown is going to hurt you son" Sifu warned

Wayne as he grabbed me and walked me outside. "Yo Ahk just go home and chill for a couple of days until everyone cools off" Sifu told me "You know how that Nigga Ted is man."

I walked outside and saw my ex-wife Zina in the parking lot with my son TJ. It was his birthday and I had promised to take him shopping and the mall was about to close in 15 minutes. I wasn't much in the mood, but we managed to make it to Toys R Us before the store closed.

The next day I had gotten phone calls from everybody at the studio asking me to come back everybody except the person who asked me to leave. Christo called Tim Smith and Markell called me. Chauncey even called. Each laying out their own plea for me to come back, but I was truly like "Fuck it".

It truly felt as if a weight had been lifted off of my shoulders no more long hours for a little pay, no more breaking bad news to good people, no more covering for this guy.

I quickly got a regular job as a junior developer for a software development company making $56,000 a year and only working 8 hours a day. Before long I started a label called Felony Records. I had Teddy's black sheep cousin Pookie and a few other producers on board and even former Teddy protégée Mike Etheridge was interested in working with me post future.

I had developed a relationship with entertainment attorney Louise West, the same entertainment attorney who help Jay Z and Dame Dash start Rockafella. Louise started a distribution company and invested $150,000 in us to do Troy's debut album as Jason Alias. We released the 1st single

"Party All Night" but before we could start to promote it Troy jumped out the window for a few bucks with some fake ass competitors called "Black Russian Records" their label eventually got raided by the Feds and I stressed about paying Louise back the money she had invested thus far.

"Tony don't stress it ...it was an investment not a loan" that eased my mind and made me love that lady even more. There is nothing I wouldn't do for Louise.

That's the thing about not burning bridges and not wearing out your welcome.

My best and dearest friends were made between 1991 and 1998 at Future Recording Studios. Guys who I can pick up the phone and call and we pick up like we talked yesterday.

We all have the common saying that Teddy brought us all together and built an unbreakable brotherhood of sorts. After I left I maintained contact with most of the people I had met while working there.

I keep in touch with artists like Lamenga, Chance MC, Mike Etheridge and a few others. Over the years unfortunately I lost a few close friends from Future like Al Davidson, Will Skylz Stewart, Rodeo Ralph, Daryl Dezo Adams and Teddy Blend, but I'm thankful for the relationships that have been maintained with friends like Sprague Williams, Tim Smith, Walter Mucho Scott, Julius "Pookie" MCKelvey, Keivan Williams, Christo Washington, Keivan Williams, George Junior Mayers, Serban Ghena, John Haynes, Earl Thomas, Tony Sifu Watts men who I am proud to call my brothers. And my sister Kareen Linton, Nicole Rembert-Riley, Donna Roberts, Lamenga Kafi, Lynese "QueenPen" Walters, Karen

Anderson, and Sherry Blair.

These wonderful people were all part of the hidden elements behind the hits. Their energies contributed to the inspirational atmosphere that made Future Recording Studios one of the most magical places I've ever experienced.

To watch Teddy Riley start a song from an idea where he is just silently nodding his head is truly fascinating...you will actually start to nod with him even though there is no music playing at all..then as he layers the drum tracks you can just feel the funk starting to grow, Teddy is very particular in his drum sounds and as he adds various elements to the beat the idea begins to manifest, the next instrument takes you to a whole different vibe.

Just when you think you know where he is going with the melody he'll surprise your ear with lush chords and pads and by the time the music portion of the song is done you feel this sense of anxiousness to hear the lyrics. I feel blessed to have witnessed the creative processes of this musical master and so many legends and musical geniuses.

I thank GOD for every opportunity presented to me. Many hits songs were born at 4338 Virginia Beach Blvd.

Chapter 21

Keep Your Receipts

For the majority of my time at future recording studios I had been under a court order to pay child support to my ex-wife Zina. One day a few years after I left Future, I had received a check for $20,000 for some freelance work I had done for a client.

I deposited the check into my bank account on a Friday and the following Monday I went to make a withdrawal to find out that $14,000 of my money had been intercepted by the Division of Child

Support Services for back Child support payments.

I went crazy trying to figure out what the fuck happened to my money as far as I knew all of my child support had been paid and I wasn't late or behind on anything. I contacted the agency to try and get to the bottom of the problem. The young lady who helped me find out how the money was missing also instigated more anger as she explained to me "between the years of 1996 and 1998 we do not have any record of any payments" she explained.

That's crazy the money was being taken directly out of my paychecks I explained to her. "Well I recommend getting a lawyer and getting in contact with the employer" she explained. Now the dilemma I faced was that Teddy had already left Virginia. The studio was still in Virginia Beach and in jeopardy of foreclosure, but nobody would tell me where Teddy was.

I was able to find all of my old pay stubs and take them into DCSE to try and prove that the payments had been deducted from my check, but that still wasn't enough proof for them. Because their ledger did not show any payments coming in, despite the dates of my deductions corresponding to the dates that the payments were due I was fucked out of $14,000 by the Commonwealth of Virginia because some dumb ass in Teddy's camp wasn't sending the payments they deducted from me into DCSE.

I needed a laywer, I had to suc. "You want me to sue Teddy Riley for your child support?" the first lawyer I went to see was so star struck she couldn't get past the job ..."So what was it like working for Teddy"..."Who were some of the people you met?" She was asking all of the wrong questions to help me get my money back.

I eventually filed a lawsuit in Federal court, because Teddy's business had relocated out of Virginia. Filing a lawsuit was easy but finding him to serve him was difficult until...my homeboy Hootie Bang told me Teddy is doing a show in Norfolk at the ODU Ted Constant Center with GUY.

I caught up with and hung out with Aaron Hall all that day and when it was time for him to do the show we left his hotel room and I rode to the stadium with him and Bang. Once backstage I ran into Teddy who initially seemed happy to see me we hugged and he introduced me to his then wife "Yo TB I want you to meet my wife Melinda, she used to date Usher" Teddy proudly introduced his trophy wife Melinda Santiago to me and I thought to myself "what? you got married to someone other than Donna and what a weird way to introduce your wife." I wanted to give him the papers as soon as I saw him but he was about to go on stage and I didn't want to fuck up his vibe so I waited around.

After GUY came off stage I caught up with Teddy again as he was talking to some fans backstage. I interrupted "yo Teddy I need to give you something" I said as I slid the court documents to him..."it's business nothing personal" I said to him as I walked away. "Call me man let's talk about this?" I didn't want to file a lawsuit against Teddy, but I couldn't afford to have $14k taken from me and from my kids.

I know Teddy himself didn't take the money from me. He had always been fair with me moneywise, but it was his company, the accountants and bookkeepers worked for him and as a result he was ultimately responsible for what happened.

I waited for a call but Teddy never reached out to me himself, instead he lawyered up and somehow the case was dismissed from Federal court.

I think it was an issue with the way the suit was filed. That caused me to go crazy and I thought to myself if I ain't getting my money through the court Imma have to get it through the street.

I went to Future Recording Studio with the intention to take $14,000 worth of his shit to make up for the money that had been taken from me. Earl was left at the studio.

I think Earl was actually living in the building at the time waiting for the foreclosure to go through. He was barricaded inside with the doors locked and the steel security gate lowered. I rang the doorbell and Earl initially tried to act as if he wasn't there. I continued to frantically ring the bell knowing Earl was in the building but he never answered the door. I hit the hidden switch on the outside of the studio that opens the steel gate and as the gate is raising up Earl comes to the door..."TB wah gone star?" Teddy said don't let nobody in here."

I pushed past Earl and went into the A-Room and started unhooking equipment..."Tone c'mon now man Teddy gonna get me" Earl pleaded with me to stop taking gear. He called Teddy "Yo Chief Tony Brown up here Mon going crazy" There wasn't even $14,000 worth of shit left in the studio for real. The keyboards and gear I was removing was worth a few thousand bucks at best. As I step outside carrying a Yamaha keyboard, I see Hootie Bang pulling up. "Yo Tony Teddy just called me man" Bang started to say but I interrupted "Oh yeah and what the fuck you supposed to do?" I said squaring up to take on Bang. "I'm here to keep your ass outta jail lil bro" Band said "You know they aint gonna do nothing, but call the police next bro come on, this nigga aint even got $14,000 right now bro."

Bang talked me down some. I had my man Tabari parked across the street with the guns pointed my way to watch my back, I signaled for him to come over. Bang was our boy so we weren't going to do anything to him, but I was so frustrated that I slammed the keyboard down onto the concrete shattering it into pieces and then left with Bang and Tabari.

A few months later the Division of Child Support Services contacted me and told me, because I had all of my paystubs and proof of payments, that they would be picking the case up and summoned

Teddy to appear in court in the city of Chesapeake Virginia. Teddy showed up in court with 2 security guys, Bull and Ricco, mean mugging me the whole time. I knew Bull because his father was a gospel singer and I used to book his dad's group for gigs years earlier. His dad and I became cool and I knew Bull when he was a kid. I didn't know nor give a fuck about the other guy.

Teddy's lawyers stated in court that Mr. Riley's financial records which were kept by his accountant Michael Mitnick were destroyed in the 911 World Trade Center Bombing… how convenient.

The case was continued and Teddy walked out of the courtroom with a smug look on his face. When the preceding was over I made my way into the hallway and greeted Bull by slapping him on his chest and asking him "How you daddy doing" that was my way of telling Teddy fuck your security, Bull smiled and said "He's doing fine" a court deputy sensed the tension and came out into the hall way to circumvent anything.

At the following hearing Teddy was a no show and the case was continued on 2 more occasions. I had actually given up and just chalked it up as a loss.

After all, who was I NOT to get fucked over by Teddy? Junior was one of my best friends and Teddy screwed him out of months of income, in fact all of the engineers got screwed out of months of pay and each of them had left Future Recording Studios bitter. Most of the artists left feeling they were owed money or at least an opportunity to fulfill their recording obligation. I was cool with most everyone there, even those who would come and go over the years and most everyone would confide in me at some point telling me about money Teddy owed them or how he screwed them out of money.

I knew first hand about some of the broken financial promises, like people being promised a certain amount per show but then only getting that amount per week. "Teddy never did me like that man, are you sure you understood his offer?" I would try to take up for him but damn it finally happened to me. SO I just ate it as a loss.

Chapter 22

It's All Over Baby

I went home from work one day and checked my mailbox to find an envelope from DCSE..."What the fuck do they want now" I thought to myself all of my kids were grown and over 18 by now I KNOW they cant still be trying to get money from me.

I was just about to rip the envelope in half when a calmness came over me and instead I opened the envelope to find a refund check for $14,800.00. I examined the check in disbelief and read the attached letter explaining how the original funds were tracked down and I was being refunded for an overpayment.

I sat down and actually cried. It was a cry of relief from all of the phone calls court dates arguments and stress of driving without a license…yeah in Virginia they would suspend your driver's license for delinquent child support payments, I spent 2 years riding dirty without a license. So it was a cry of thanks to GOD.

I felt as if my tenacity had been rewarded. Two days later, I turned on my television set to the news and heard the news reporter announcing "Singer Teddy Riley's Virginia Beach Recording Studio Burns Down After Being Struck By Lightning" I couldn't believe it.

I hopped in my car and drove to the location of the studio. When I arrived, my eyes were in disbelief.

It was horrific!

The top of the building was badly burned and the studio had been damaged to the point it had to be condemned. Future Recording Studios would be no more.

I reflected on all of the icons who walked through that building and all of the legendary songs that came out of there. A spot where GOD once rained down musical magic was destroyed when he decided to rain down fiery lightning.

Although it had taken me about 6 years after my last day at Future Recording Studios to rectify the only problem I ever had with Teddy I never wanted to see the building totally destroyed. In hindsight many of the artists and employees of Future Recording Studios between 1991 and 1998 had their hope dreams destroyed, maybe it was reciprocity in the form of a bolt of lightning.

Since then the group Blackstreet has undergone as many personnel changes as the Temptations. Joe Stomestreet, Dave Hollister, Levi Little, Mark Middleton and Terrell Phillips were all pulled into and let go from one of the most noted R&B groups of the 90s. Eric Williams has seemed to remain a stable fixture since he joined the group, but It was strange to see Teddy and Chauncey split ways. They had the Black Pinky bond and seemed unshakeable but things got ugly.

When Chauncy left Blackstreet to go sign with Busta Rhymes Flipmode squad I feared that it was all over. Teddy started touring with a group of guys he called BS2 and I call karaoke singers while Chauncey, Eric, Levi and Mark joined forces as the voices of Blackstreet (minus Dave) and all bonded together to tour as Blackstreet. Somehow, the trademark period for the name had expired and no one on Teddy's team at the time thought to stay on top of the paperwork to renew the trademark.

Chauncy was very clever to swoop in and secure the trademark of the name so that he and the other guys could continue to tour under the name Blackstreet. It's sad that Teddy doesn't seem to have anyone paying attention to his affairs. He has lost several storage rooms that I used to maintain while I was manager, because someone neglected to pay the rental fee for the storage unit. As a result priceless musical artifacts were lost.

Master reels from Michael Jackson, GUY and more, Touring costumes from GUY such as those rhinestone airbrushed jackets and even the motorcycle used in the "Baby Be Mine" video were auctioned off to the highest bidder.

A few years later tapes of Michael Jackson's

unfinished songs and raw vocals would begin to pop up over the internet.

In February of 2021, I went to Hampton Virginia to BlackLabel Recording Studios which is co-owned by Blake and Chauncey to check out a few tracks from the new Blackstreet album which is being produced by Mucho's nephew J-HOT. I was very delighted with the new musical offerings the group was preparing to release. I had a chance to catch up with Mark and Eric but because of the COVID restriction we kept our distance but expressed our affection and admiration for each other.

Chauncey has masterminded a brilliant comeback for Blackstreet, without the production efforts of Teddy, but their audience and fans shouldn't be too upset, the songs I previewed were fantastic and a few surprises are in store for fans of New

Jack Swing and 90s era music.

The last time I saw Teddy was in 2019 at "Something In The Water" Festival. After a brief second of hesitancy on both of our parts we hugged and greeted each other and began to catch up on the good things that have happened in both of our lives over time.

I also caught up with Pharrel that day and did something I had never asked any celebrity that came through the doors of Future "Can We get a picture together?" While posing for the photo I said to Pharrell. "I'm proud of you bro...you were worrisome back in the day." "Worrisome?" Pharrell replied "Yeah as a motherfucker but look at what that allowed you to accomplish."

I introduced Skateboard P to my youngest son Cameron who is an aspiring MC himself and my "COOL DAD" points instantly increased by

100%.

Later that day Teddy and his daughters Deja and Taja along with Hootie Bang, my son Cameron and myself had lunch together at MacArthur Mall in downtown Norfolk.

There were a few other fans/friends who were present and it ended up being a wonderful moment in time. I felt at ease.. it wasn't like the old days, but it was good to let go of the resentment that had built up over the years.

 "Teddy, I started out "You know I never took a photo with you the whole time I've known you" "Let's take one now" Teddy replied. I passed my cell phone to Hootie Bang, Teddy and I posed for a flick and that was that.

THE END

IN MEMORIUM OF THOSE I MET AT FUTURE

WHO ARE NO LONGER WITH US

ALLEN "BIG AL" DAVIDSON

DARYL "DEZO" ADAMS

WILL "SKYLZ" STEWART

TEDDY BLENDZ

OMAR CHANDLER

JOSEPH STONESTREET

DONNA MOORE

DEAUTHUR DIXON

RALPH "RODEO" THOROUGOOD

RUSSEL "OL DIRTY BASTARD" JONES CHRISTOPHER

"BIGGIE SMALLS" WALLACE

CRAIG MACK

MAYOR MYERA ORBENDORF

MICHAEL JACKSON

WHITNEY HOUSTON

Published by

ASSERTIVE MULTIMEDIA LLC

© 2021 Assertive Multimedia LLC

ALL RIGHTS RESERVED

www.ingramcontent.com/pod-product-compliance
Lightning Source LLC
Chambersburg PA
CBHW071658170426
43195CB00039B/2232